Mama now cooks like this!

Mama *now cooks like this!*

THE BEST OF
Susan Mendelson

whitecap

SUSAN MENDELSON has been writing cookbooks since 1979 when she founded her catering company, The Lazy Gourmet. Over the years she has shared her recipes on radio, television and in her nine previous books that preceded *Mama Now Cooks Like This*.

To Jack.

For additional information, contact Whitecap Books Ltd., 351 Lynn Avenue, North Vancouver, BC, V7J 2C4. Visit our website at www.whitecap.ca.

LIBRARY AND ARCHIVES CANADA CATALOGUING IN PUBLICATION
Mendelson, Susan, 1952-
    Mama now cooks like this : the best of Susan Mendelson/ Susan Mendelson, author ; Tracy Kusiewicz, photographer.
Includes index.
ISBN 1-55285-508-2
ISBN 978-1-55285-508-9
    1. Cookery. I. Title.
TX715.M528 2006   641.5   C2006-902352-2

The publisher acknowledges the financial support of the Government of Canada through the Book Publishing Industry Development Program, and the Cultural Services Branch of the Government of British Columbia for our publishing program. Whitecap Books also acknowledges the financial support of the Province of British Columbia through the Book Publishing Tax Credit.

Editor: Viola Funk
Proofreader: Joan E. Templeton
Design: R-house/Roberta Batchelor
Pattern Illustration: Rosemary Travale
Photography: Tracy Kusiewicz
Food styling: Irene McGuinness
Prop sources:
  Chintz & Company
    950 Homer Street Van BC V6B 2W7
    Tel: 604-689-2022
    www.chintz.com
  Puddifoot Gifts & Tableware
    2375 West 41st Avenue Van BC V6M 2A3
    Tel: 604-261-8141 or 1-877-261-8141
    www.puddifoot.com
  Shed Home Furnishings
    4368 West 10th Avenue Van BC V6R 2H7
    Tel: 604-228-4368
    www.shedhomefurnishings.com
  Marrakesh Design
    2675 Arbutus Street Van BC V6J 3Y4
    Tel: 604-734-0735
    www.marrakeshdesign.com
  Chocolate Mousse Kitchenware
    1553 Robson Street Van BC V6G 1C3
    Tel: 604-682-8223
  Hollyfields Home & Garden
    1535 Johnston Street Granville Island Van BC V6H 3R9
    Tel: 604-688-2929
    www.hollyfields.ca
  Folkart Interiors
    3651 West 10th Avenue Van BC V6R 2G2
    Tel: 604-731-7576
    www.folkartinteriors.com
  Creekside Tile Company
    161 West 2nd Avenue Van BC V5Y 1B8
    Tel: 604-876-4900
    www.creeksidetile.com

Contents

Introduction

In the fall of 1980 *Mama Never Cooked Like This* emerged on the culinary scene with a print run of 7,000 copies and sold out on its first day on the shelves. The reason for this was that it was a compilation of recipes given to listeners of CBC Radio's Vancouver drive-home show over a four-year period. After each broadcast, listeners would phone in to ask the CBC to send them the recipes that I had just shared on the air.

After several years of receiving recipes, many listeners wrote to ask me to collect them all in a book. I was happy to comply but had no idea that the book would take off and appeal to such a wide audience. Those listeners created the buzz and the cookbook's astronomical success. Talon Books sent me on a national tour, and the next 15,000 copies sold out in the next six weeks, after which another 25,000 copies were printed and sold. The book had seven Canadian printings.

After St. Martin's Press in New York bought the book's American rights, I went on an American tour, during which I was privileged to experience the 15 minutes of fame available only in cities like New York and Los Angeles. The high point of my experience came one afternoon, months after I did a cooking demonstration on "Hour Magazine," an American afternoon TV show that aired nationally. I got a phone call from my grandparents in Florida (long-distance calls were a big deal in those days!). They were so excited they could barely speak! Who should show up on their favorite TV show,

but me, their own granddaughter. I had talked about dedicating my book to my grandmother Faye. That call was one of the most memorable moments of my life and career.

Two years later *Let Me in the Kitchen* was published to coincide with a song-and-dance cooking show of the same name that premiered at the Vancouver International Children's Festival. It was a dream come true, one of the highlights of my life, to perform my own show. My future husband, Jack, took his seven-year-old son, Soleil, to that show and when, six years later, he told me about being there, it endeared him to me for life!

Alas, it was to be my last stage performance, but then Deborah Roitberg—my former business partner and co-founder of The Lazy Gourmet—and I went on to become regular guests on the CKVU Friday evening show that featured our recipes. It was the early days of cooking TV, long before cooking shows were everywhere.

Deborah and I next published two cookbooks back to back: *Nuts About Chocolate* in 1983 and *Fresh Tarts* in 1985. In 1986 my *Expo '86 Souvenir Cookbook* was the only cookbook sold on the Expo site. It was an unbelievable opportunity to take my recipes all over the world. Since then I've received many letters and, more recently, emails requesting copies of that book, which has long been out of print.

Two years later, Deborah and I parted ways, but in 1992 we wrote the sequel to *Nuts About Chocolate*, called *Still Nuts About Chocolate*. My sister Rena Mendelson and I co-wrote *Food to Grow On* in 1994. Rena provided the nutritional guidelines for mothers-to-be, as well as for infants and children, and I provided the recipes to illustrate her information. Joey Cruz—my chef at the time—and I co-wrote *The Lazy Gourmet Cookbook* in 2000, with updated recipes from The Lazy Gourmet Bistro and Catering Company. Cookbook number nine was an update with my sister of *Food to Grow On*. It contained new recipes, as well as updated recipes from the previous book that increased fibre and decreased fat. It's the only one of my books still in print.

With so many of my cookbooks out of print and so many requests for the recipes, I decided to bring out a "best of" book with many of my most sought-after recipes.

It's been 26 years since the publication of *Mama Never Cooked Like This*. I'm now the mama with a 16-year-old daughter and married stepson and daughter-in-law. Although most of the time I still work full time at The Lazy Gourmet, in the summer my family spends four days a week at our lakeside home, where I experiment with new recipes and ingredients. I'm happiest when creating new food ideas for the 21st century.

My herb garden is a big part of my inspiration. I love to use fresh herbs in my summertime recipes. I've added many new recipes to this cookbook that were developed at the lake. Jewish holidays are an important part of our family life, and I've finally parted with many secret family recipes that customers have begged me to divulge for years. They're all in the book's Family Traditions section.

I'd like to end with a short anecdote. One morning, when my daughter Mira was four or five years old, she begged me to make waffles. I had things to do and suggested French toast as a quicker alternative. She whined, and finally I begrudgingly agreed to make the waffles. She then burst into tears. I said, "Mira, I said that I'd make you the waffles. Why are you crying?" She looked up with her tear-streaked face and said, "Yes, but you won't make them with love." My five year old expressed what I deeply believe: food tastes better when it's made with love. We need to keep that in mind when we make food for our loved ones.

My hope is that *Mama Now Cooks Like This* will be enjoyed as much as *Mama Never Cooked Like This* and that families will use the recipes for their daily meals, entertaining and family holidays so that they become, not Susan Mendelson recipes, but their own family favorites.

To honour my 30 years in the food business, I've chosen to donate 10 percent of all royalties to Big Sisters of BC Lower Mainland and 10 percent of all royalties to Vancouver Jewish Family Service Agency Food Programs.

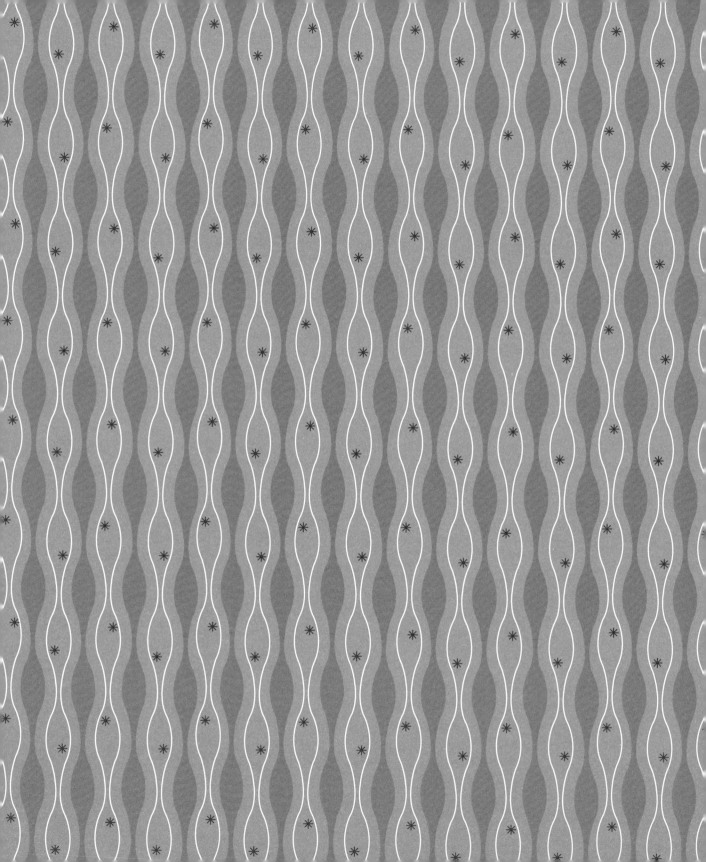

CHAPTER ONE

Hors d'oeuvres

Caviar Pie

from *Mama Never Cooked Like This*

Chill and serve with crisp sesame seed crackers. You'll wow everyone with this recipe! I developed it over 25 years ago and customers still ask for it.

1 large avocado	Mash and press into an 8- or 9-inch (20- or 23-cm) clear Pyrex pie plate.
3 Tbsp (45 mL) red onion	Chop finely and sprinkle over avocado.
6 hard-boiled eggs 2 Tbsp (30 mL) mayonnaise	Grate eggs and combine with mayonnaise. Place gently over onion layer.
one 3½-oz (100-g) jar lumpfish caviar	Spoon carefully on top.

Serves 10

Cream Cheese-Stuffed Mushroom Caps

from *Mama Never Cooked Like This*

An old-fashioned recipe that guests still love. So easy to make!

	Preheat oven to 350°F (180°C).
24 mushrooms	Stem mushrooms and remove centres.
1 cup (250 mL) spreadable cream cheese ½ cup (125 mL) shredded Swiss cheese ¼ cup (50 mL) chopped nuts	Combine ingredients and fill cavities of mushroom caps with mixture.
pineapple juice	Place in a greased baking dish and sprinkle with pineapple juice.
	Cover and bake in preheated oven for 20 minutes.

Makes 2 dozen caps

Coconut Scallops

from *The Expo 86 Cookbook*

This recipe is also fantastic made with BC prawns! The Expo cookbook has travelled all over the world and now that so many people have access to the Internet, I get wonderful messages from all over the globe about these recipes.

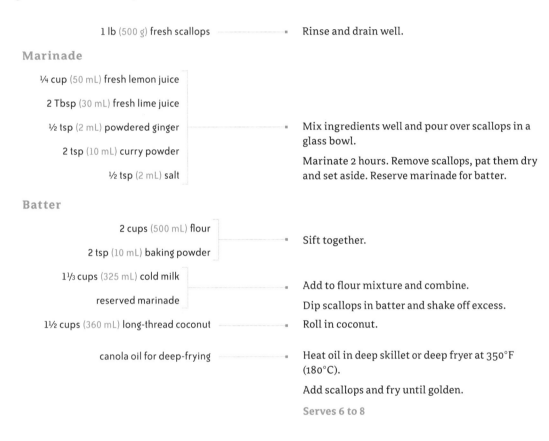

1 lb (500 g) fresh scallops — Rinse and drain well.

Marinade

¼ cup (50 mL) fresh lemon juice

2 Tbsp (30 mL) fresh lime juice

½ tsp (2 mL) powdered ginger — Mix ingredients well and pour over scallops in a glass bowl.

2 tsp (10 mL) curry powder

Marinate 2 hours. Remove scallops, pat them dry and set aside. Reserve marinade for batter.

½ tsp (2 mL) salt

Batter

2 cups (500 mL) flour — Sift together.

2 tsp (10 mL) baking powder

1⅓ cups (325 mL) cold milk — Add to flour mixture and combine.

reserved marinade — Dip scallops in batter and shake off excess.

1½ cups (360 mL) long-thread coconut — Roll in coconut.

canola oil for deep-frying — Heat oil in deep skillet or deep fryer at 350°F (180°C).

Add scallops and fry until golden.

Serves 6 to 8

Easy Brie and Pecans in Phyllo

from The Expo 86 Cookbook

Preheat oven to 400° (200°C).

1 lb (500 g) brie	Cut cheese into 24 small pieces.
½ lb (250 g) phyllo pastry	Cut sheets, one at a time, into 11- × 3-inch (28- × 8-cm) strips.
½ cup (125 mL) butter, melted	Brush each strip with melted butter.
½ cup (125 mL) chopped pecans	Sprinkle strips with nuts.

Place a piece of brie at the bottom right-hand corner of each pastry strip and form a triangle by folding the corner up to meet the opposite side, enclosing the cheese. Continue to fold the pastry in a series of diagonals, making sure that the dough is well sealed with each turn. (If not well sealed, brie may ooze out as it melts.)

tip: Try adding a small piece of apple to each pocket as well.

Place on a baking sheet and bake in preheated oven for 16 to 18 minutes until golden.

Makes 4 dozen phyllo triangles

Goat Cheese (Chèvre) Spread

from Food to Grow On

A simple but very tasty spread. Great for people who can't tolerate cow's milk.

⅓ cup (75 mL) sun-dried tomatoes	Soak tomatoes in water. Let sit for 5 minutes, drain and pat dry.
⅓ cup (75 mL) boiling water	
8 oz (250 g) goat cheese [chèvre]	Mix in food processor with tomatoes.
4 cloves garlic, minced	

Serve in a bowl, with whole wheat baguette rounds or toast.

Serves 4

Camembert-en-Croûte

from *The Expo 86 Cookbook*

Could it be any easier?
This *croûte* can be made different sizes, depending on the number of people you wish to serve.

Preheat the oven to 400°F (200°C).

puff pastry ⋯⋯⋯⋯⋯⋯⋯⋯ ▪ On lightly floured board, roll out pastry until it is 1 inch (2.5 cm) larger than round of cheese (see exact amounts below).

1 wheel Camembert or brie ⋯⋯ ▪ Place cheese on pastry.

1 egg, beaten ⋯⋯⋯⋯⋯ ▪ Brush protruding rim of pastry with egg wash. Top with a larger round of pastry. With small paring knife or kitchen shears, trim top pastry to meet bottom pastry evenly.

Crimp bottom and top crusts by pressing together. Use excess pastry pieces to decorate *croûte*. Brush with egg wash.

tip: Check occasionally while baking to make sure the cheese does not seep out. If it does, remove *croûte* from oven. Let the cheese sit until almost firm, then cut off part of the top, scoop the cheese back in and replace the top. Your guests will never know and your party will be rescued.

Bake in preheated oven until outside is puffy, crisp and golden brown: 15 minutes for 5-oz (142-mL) wheel; 20 to 22 minutes for 2-lb (1-kg) wheel; 25 to 30 minutes for 5-lb (2.2-kg) wheel.

Serves 3 to 4

¼ lb (125 g) puff pastry

one 5-oz (142-mL) wheel of Camembert or brie

variations: Try topping the cheese with fresh blueberries and a sprinkling of sugar before covering with the crust. A sprinkling of brown sugar and pecans also makes a delicious topping for the cheese. Have fun experimenting with this recipe.

Serves 12 to 15

10 oz (284 g) puff pastry

one 2-lb (1-kg) wheel of Camembert or brie

Serves 35 or more

2 lb (1 kg) puff pastry

one 5-lb (2.2-kg) wheel of Camembert or brie

Lazy Gourmet Lox Mousse

from The Expo 86 Cookbook

Enjoy our BC smoked salmon: keep it up to one year in your freezer and indulge in the flavours of Vancouver year-round. My friend Roberta Nieman first made this for me in 1973. I had never liked lox before, but I loved this spread.

1 lb (500 g) spreadable cream cheese

2 tsp (10 mL) lemon juice

3–4 oz (75–125 g) smoked salmon [lox]

freshly ground pepper to taste

In a food processor or with an electric mixer, purée until well blended.

Serve on bagels, pumpernickel or sesame crackers.

Serves 10

Saffron Mussels

from Food to Grow On

Makes a perfect light summer dinner as well!

½ cup (125 mL) chopped onion

2 cloves garlic, minced

1 Tbsp (15 mL) olive oil

Sauté onion and garlic in oil until soft.

1 cup (250 mL) chopped tomatoes

½ cup (125 mL) white wine

½ cup (125 mL) water

½ tsp (2 mL) saffron

Add to onion and let simmer for 5 minutes.

2 lb (1 kg) mussels

Add to wine mixture and cover. Steam for 5 to 7 minutes, or until mussels open. Discard unopened mussels.

Serve with crusty bread.

Serves 2

Triple Bell Pepper and Onion Quesadillas

from *Food to Grow On*

Quesadillas are wonderful for lunch as well as for appetizers. I now look for multigrain tortillas and often add vegetables that are leftover from a previous meal.

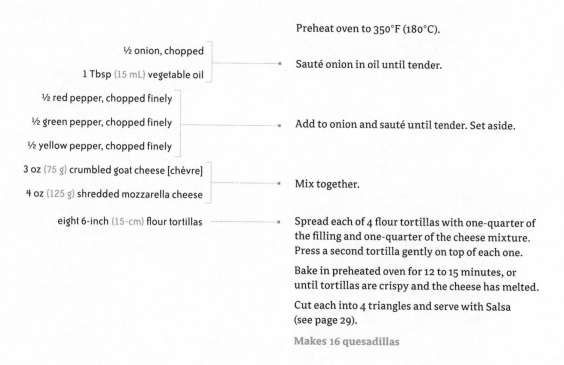

Preheat oven to 350°F (180°C).

½ onion, chopped
1 Tbsp (15 mL) vegetable oil

Sauté onion in oil until tender.

½ red pepper, chopped finely
½ green pepper, chopped finely
½ yellow pepper, chopped finely

Add to onion and sauté until tender. Set aside.

3 oz (75 g) crumbled goat cheese [chèvre]
4 oz (125 g) shredded mozzarella cheese

Mix together.

eight 6-inch (15-cm) flour tortillas

Spread each of 4 flour tortillas with one-quarter of the filling and one-quarter of the cheese mixture. Press a second tortilla gently on top of each one.

Bake in preheated oven for 12 to 15 minutes, or until tortillas are crispy and the cheese has melted.

Cut each into 4 triangles and serve with Salsa (see page 29).

Makes 16 quesadillas

Mushroom Nut Paté

from *Food to Grow On*

This is a favorite paté for vegetarians. I always label it clearly to warn those who may have nut allergies.

Preheat oven to 350°F (180°C).

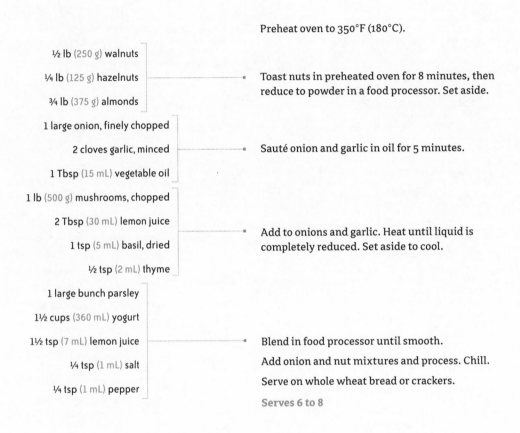

½ lb (250 g) walnuts
¼ lb (125 g) hazelnuts
¾ lb (375 g) almonds

Toast nuts in preheated oven for 8 minutes, then reduce to powder in a food processor. Set aside.

1 large onion, finely chopped
2 cloves garlic, minced
1 Tbsp (15 mL) vegetable oil

Sauté onion and garlic in oil for 5 minutes.

1 lb (500 g) mushrooms, chopped
2 Tbsp (30 mL) lemon juice
1 tsp (5 mL) basil, dried
½ tsp (2 mL) thyme

Add to onions and garlic. Heat until liquid is completely reduced. Set aside to cool.

1 large bunch parsley
1½ cups (360 mL) yogurt
1½ tsp (7 mL) lemon juice
¼ tsp (1 mL) salt
¼ tsp (1 mL) pepper

Blend in food processor until smooth.

Add onion and nut mixtures and process. Chill.

Serve on whole wheat bread or crackers.

Serves 6 to 8

Wild Mushroom Risotto Balls

These risotto balls melt in your mouth when served warm. I also make larger ones to serve as a side dish with fish or chicken.

3 cups (750 mL) vegetable broth	Heat until broth is simmering. Reduce to low.
2 Tbsp (30 mL) olive oil	
½ cup (125 mL) finely chopped onion	In medium saucepan, heat oil. Sauté onions and mushrooms until soft (about 5 minutes).
1 cup (250 mL) assorted mushrooms, sliced	
1 cup (250 mL) plus 2 Tbsp (30 mL) arborio rice	Add rice. Stir 1 minute.
¼ cup (50 mL) dry white wine	Add wine and stir until absorbed.
	Add broth one-third at a time and simmer until rice is just tender and risotto is creamy, allowing broth to be completely absorbed before adding more, and stirring often (this will take about 18 minutes). Remove from heat.
6 Tbsp (90 mL) grated Parmesan cheese	Add grated cheese and butter.
2 Tbsp (30 mL) butter	
salt and pepper	Season to taste.
	Spread onto 13- × 9-inch (33- × 23-cm) pan and cool completely.
6 oz (175 g) fontina cheese, cubed	Shape risotto into 1-inch (2.5-cm) balls, placing a small cube of fontina in the centre of each ball. Place on small plate.
2 eggs	Beat eggs in a shallow bowl.
1½ cups (360 g) *panko* [Japanese breadcrumbs]	Dip risotto ball into beaten egg, then into *panko* to coat.
	Preheat oven to 300°F (160°C).
canola oil for frying	In large shallow skillet, heat oil to medium-high heat and sauté risotto balls until crisp and brown. Transfer to baking sheet to keep warm in preheated oven.

Makes 36 to 40 balls

Chèvre with Pesto

from *Food to Grow On*

Thanks to my sister Rena for giving me this recipe. It's always the first spread to disappear at a party!

6 oz (175 g) chèvre, formed into a ball

1 Tbsp (15 mL) olive oil

Roll cheese in oil.

¼ cup (50 mL) chopped pecans

¼ cup (50 mL) mustard seeds

1 Tbsp (15mL) coarsely ground black pepper

Mix pecans, mustard seeds and pepper together. Roll cheese in pecan mixture.

one 10-oz (284-mL) package frozen spinach, thawed

½ cup (125 mL) pesto sauce [recipe follows, or use store-bought]

1 Tbsp (15 mL) rice vinegar

Blend spinach, pesto and vinegar in a food processor.

Preheat oven to 400°F (200°C).

3 Tbsp (45 mL) olive oil

Grease a 13- × 9-inch (3.5-L) casserole dish with olive oil.

Place spinach mixture in prepared casserole dish. Spread to edges.

Heat cheese in oven for 4 to 5 minutes. Carefully place cheese on spinach mixture. The spinach mixture can be warmed in a microwave for 20 seconds on medium.

Serves 2 to 4

Pesto

from *The Lazy Gourmet*

I felt that I had discovered a new world when I discovered pesto. I hope you love it too!

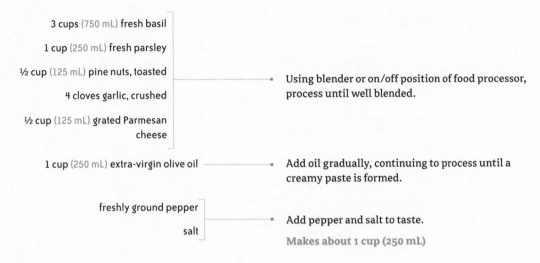

3 cups (750 mL) fresh basil

1 cup (250 mL) fresh parsley

½ cup (125 mL) pine nuts, toasted

4 cloves garlic, crushed

½ cup (125 mL) grated Parmesan cheese

Using blender or on/off position of food processor, process until well blended.

1 cup (250 mL) extra-virgin olive oil

Add oil gradually, continuing to process until a creamy paste is formed.

freshly ground pepper

salt

Add pepper and salt to taste.

Makes about 1 cup (250 mL)

tip: Pesto is a marvelous addition to soups and sauces, and it freezes well. When fresh basil is available, make extra for future use.

Crab Cakes *with* Tropical Fruit Salsa

from *Food to Grow On*

Make these crab cakes for a main course as well as for appetizers.

1 lb (500 g) crab, preferably Dungeness

1 egg

¼ cup (50 mL) chopped sweet onion

¼ cup (50 mL) chopped celery

¼ cup (50 mL) *panko*
[Japanese breadcrumbs]

2 Tbsp (30 mL) mayonnaise — Mix together and form patties.

1 Tbsp (15 mL) Dijon mustard

2 dashes of Tabasco

juice of 1 lemon

¼ tsp (1 mL) salt

¼ tsp (1 mL) pepper

½ cup (125 mL) *panko*
[Japanese breadcrumbs] [optional] — Dip patties into crumbs if desired.

small amount of canola oil or butter — Preheat oil in a frying pan and fit patties into pan. Cook until medium brown on both sides.

Serve with Tropical Fruit Salsa (recipe follows).

Serves 4 to 6

Tropical Fruit Salsa

½ cup (125 mL) diced pineapple

½ cup (125 mL) diced mango

½ cup (125 mL) diced apples

½ cup (125 mL) diced strawberries

½ cup (125 mL) diced red or
yellow bell pepper

2 Tbsp (30 mL) rice vinegar

1 Tbsp (15 mL) minced cilantro

1 Tbsp (15 mL) sugar

¼ tsp (1 mL) crushed red pepper [optional]

Combine in a bowl. Refrigerate until ready to serve.

Makes 1½ cups

variations: Feel free to play with the combination of fruits in the salsa, and to use your own favorites. I have substituted half-the-fat mayonnaise in this recipe, too.

Prawn Potstickers with Ponzu Sauce

A friend and I took a cooking class from Trevor Hopper, who had a wonderful restaurant in Vancouver called Raku. Trevor shared this amazing recipe with us and we've been making it ever since.

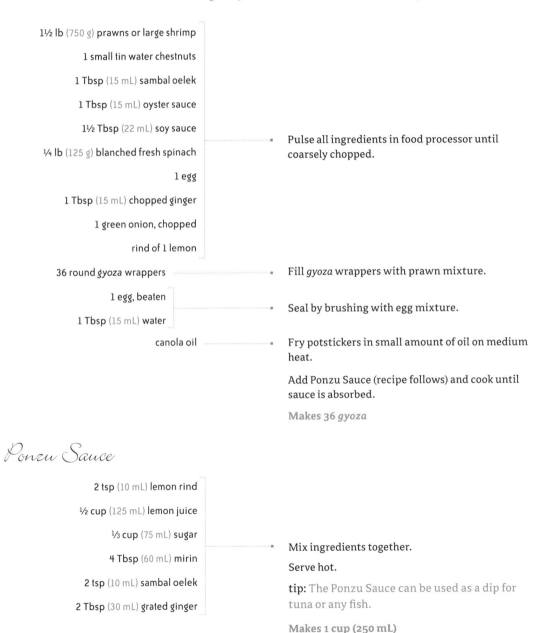

1½ lb (750 g) prawns or large shrimp

1 small tin water chestnuts

1 Tbsp (15 mL) sambal oelek

1 Tbsp (15 mL) oyster sauce

1½ Tbsp (22 mL) soy sauce

¼ lb (125 g) blanched fresh spinach

1 egg

1 Tbsp (15 mL) chopped ginger

1 green onion, chopped

rind of 1 lemon

Pulse all ingredients in food processor until coarsely chopped.

36 round *gyoza* wrappers

Fill *gyoza* wrappers with prawn mixture.

1 egg, beaten

1 Tbsp (15 mL) water

Seal by brushing with egg mixture.

canola oil

Fry potstickers in small amount of oil on medium heat.

Add Ponzu Sauce (recipe follows) and cook until sauce is absorbed.

Makes 36 *gyoza*

Ponzu Sauce

2 tsp (10 mL) lemon rind

½ cup (125 mL) lemon juice

⅓ cup (75 mL) sugar

4 Tbsp (60 mL) mirin

2 tsp (10 mL) sambal oelek

2 Tbsp (30 mL) grated ginger

Mix ingredients together.

Serve hot.

tip: The Ponzu Sauce can be used as a dip for tuna or any fish.

Makes 1 cup (250 mL)

Brie-en-Croûte with Reduced Maple Syrup and Toasted Walnuts

from *The Lazy Gourmet*

This is the current rendition of Brie-en-Croûte for cocktail parties catered by The Lazy Gourmet.

1 lb (500 g) puff pastry

Divide puff pastry into 2 balls. Roll each ball out to ¼ inch (5 mm) thick and 15 inches (38 cm) in diameter.

1 egg

2 Tbsp (30 mL) water

Whisk egg and water together to make an egg wash.

Brush 1 sheet of pastry with the egg wash.

2 lb (900 g) brie cheese

Place brie on top of one of the pastry rounds and brush with egg wash. Place a second sheet of puff pastry on top of brie. Wrap sides up and over the cheese. Decorate with extra puff pastry by shaping or cutting out designs. Brush top and sides of pastry with egg wash. Place in freezer for 1 hour.

Preheat the oven to 400°F (200°C).

Bake brie for 30 to 45 minutes, or until pastry is golden brown.

1 cup (250 mL) maple syrup

½ cup (125 mL) walnuts, coarsely chopped

In a small pot, combine maple syrup and walnuts. Bring to a boil, then turn down to a low simmer. Reduce to obtain a consistency similar to that of liquid honey.

Place baked brie on a serving platter. Pour maple syrup and walnuts over and around brie.

Serves 15 to 20

Hoppa Rolls

Another recipe from Trevor Hopper's sadly defunct Raku restaurant. You will have guests fighting over these! I promise they're worth the work.

Rice Flour Crêpe

1⅔ cups (400 mL) coconut milk

5 eggs

½ cup (125 mL) rice flour

½ cup (125 mL) white flour

½ tsp (2 mL) sea salt

Mix all ingredients.

In crêpe pan, on medium heat, make thin crêpes, one at a time.

Sauce

1 cup (250 mL) pickled ginger with juice

3 cloves garlic

1 jalapeño pepper

one ½-inch (1-cm) piece of fresh ginger, peeled

1 Tbsp (15 mL) sambal badjak

¼ cup (50 mL) rice vinegar

¾ cup (175 mL) canola oil

1 bunch cilantro

Place all ingredients in blender and mix until a beautiful green colour.

4–5 cups (1 L–1.25 L) mixed greens

1 lb (500 g) cooked shrimp, crab or salmon

1 bunch Thai basil leaves

2 avocados, sliced

On table top, place 1 crêpe.

Along the edge place ¼ cup (50 mL) of greens.

Lay 3 shrimp or equivalent amount of other seafood on top of greens.

Top with 2 to 3 leaves of Thai basil and 2 slices of avocado.

Place 2–3 Tbsp (30–45 mL) of pickled ginger sauce over the mixture. Fold edges over and roll into flat crêpe or make into a roll, ensuring that the edges are tightly sealed.

Slice into thirds and put onto appetizer buffet with small plates.

Makes 16 rolls

Almond Pine Cone Spread

from *The Lazy Gourmet*

This is gorgeous as a year-round appetizer, but at The Lazy Gourmet we only make it in December for Christmas parties.

Preheat the oven to 350°F (180°C).

3 cups (750 mL) whole blanched almonds

Toast almonds on baking sheets in preheated oven for 12 minutes, watching closely to ensure they don't burn, then cool.

1 lb (500 g) spreadable cream cheese

2 oz (50 g) blue cheese

2 oz (50 g) chèvre

½ cup (125 mL) capers, chopped

½ cup (125 mL) finely diced red onion

1 Tbsp (15 mL) brandy

Combine and mix until well blended.

Shape into a pine cone.

Starting from the bottom, insert almonds at a slight angle, forming neat rows so that it looks like one large pine cone.

Serve with crackers or sliced baguettes.

Serves 8

Chèvre and Sun-Dried Tomato Phyllo Purses

from The Lazy Gourmet

1 cup (250 mL) sun-dried tomatoes, roughly chopped

1 cup (250 mL) spreadable cream cheese

½ lightly whisked egg

¼ cup (50mL) chèvre

one 1-lb (454-g) package phyllo pastry, thawed

olive oil

In a bowl, mix together sun-dried tomatoes, cream cheese, egg and chèvre.

Lay 1 sheet of phyllo lengthwise on a clean surface. Brush with olive oil.

Lay a second sheet on top and brush with olive oil, then a third sheet and brush with olive oil.

Cut the sheets in half horizontally and vertically to create 4 rectangular sheets.

Then cut each sheet in 3 even columns, for a total of 12 columns.

Place ½–1 tsp (2–5 mL) of the chèvre mixture at the bottom of each phyllo column. Fold the right corner to the left side of the phyllo column to form a triangle.

Fold the triangle upwards.

Then fold the left corner to the right side of the sheet again, forming a triangle.

Fold the triangle upwards, and continue repeating the process until you reach the top of the phyllo column and a triangular purse is formed. Repeat with the remaining phyllo and filling.

Preheat the oven to 400°F (200°C).

Brush the top of each purse with olive oil and place on baking sheets for 10 to 12 minutes, until golden brown.

Makes 5 to 6 dozen purses

tip: Once you get the hang of phyllo, it is very easy to work with. Just remember to keep it covered with a damp tea towel when you're not working with it, as it tends to dry out very quickly. Cook only as many of these hors d'oeuvres as you can use. Freeze leftover unbaked phyllo purses and pull them out to bake when company arrives unexpectedly. Just place the frozen phyllo purses into a preheated oven.

Vietnamese Salad Rolls with Peanut Hoisin Sauce

from *The Lazy Gourmet*

8 cups (2 L) water

Bring water to a boil in a large pot.

½ bag thin rice vermicelli noodles

Add the rice noodles. Stir and cook for 5 to 8 minutes. Drain and rinse with cold running water. Using a pair of scissors, roughly cut up the noodles. Set aside.

24 rice papers, triangular shaped

Immerse 3 to 4 rice papers in warm water for 30 seconds. Remove and lay rice papers on a clean surface, pointed side away from you.

½ cup (125 mL) grated carrot

1 cup (250 mL) shredded lettuce

1 whole papaya or mango, cut into ½-inch (1-cm) strips

Place a pinch of rice noodles, carrots, lettuce and papaya or mango on the wide end of the rice paper. Fold the sides over the filling. Fold the bottom of the rice paper over the filling.

8 green onions, cut into 3-inch (8-cm) pieces

Insert a piece of green onion along the edge of the fold, allowing it to stick out of the roll.

Continue folding over to seal. Place on a serving plate.

Repeat with the remaining rice papers and filling.

Makes 2 dozen

Peanut Hoisin Sauce

1 medium onion, cut into ¼-inch (5-mm) dice

2 cloves garlic

2 Tbsp (30 mL) vegetable oil

In a saucepan over low-medium heat, sauté the onion and garlic in the oil.

2 Tbsp (30 mL) sambal oelek [available in Asian markets]

2 Tbsp (30 mL) lemon juice

2 Tbsp (30 mL) soy sauce

½ cup (125 mL) peanut butter [use a smooth, unsweetened type]

3 Tbsp (45 mL) *ketjap manis* [sweet soy sauce available in Asian markets]

3 Tbsp (45 mL) hoisin sauce

½–¾ cup (125–175 mL) hot water

Whisk in the sambal oelek, lemon juice, soy sauce, peanut butter, *ketjap manis* and hoisin sauce. Whisk in ½ cup (125 mL) of the hot water, and bring to a boil. If the consistency is too thick for dipping, whisk in enough water to thin it out. Sauce can be stored in the fridge for up to 2 weeks.

tip: Feel free to add shrimp, chicken or crab in the rolls, or experiment with the vegetables and proteins in your fridge to make interesting rolls and use up leftovers. The rice papers and hoisin sauce are available in the Asian section of most grocery stores.

Makes 2 cups (500 mL)

Quesadillas with Three Fillings

from *The Lazy Gourmet*

The beauty of quesadillas is that once you know how to make them you can put anything you want into them. I've found multigrain tortillas at Costco—they're delicious and very nutritious!

Preheat the oven to 375°F (190°C).

twenty-four 6-inch (15-cm) soft tortillas

Lay 12 tortillas on a clean surface.

1 egg

2 Tbsp (30 mL) water

Combine egg and water and brush the egg wash on the tortillas with a pastry brush.

1 recipe filling [3 choices below]

Evenly distribute your choice of filling, up to 6 Tbsp (90 mL), on each tortilla.

Brush the other 12 tortillas with egg wash and place on top of the filled tortillas. Press down to flatten the filling.

Spray a baking sheet with vegetable spray, or oil lightly. Place quesadillas on the sheet and bake for 10 to 15 minutes, until the edges are slightly browned.

Cut each tortilla into 4 wedges.

1 recipe Salsa [recipe follows]

Serve with Salsa, sour cream and guacamole.

Triple Cheese Filling

1½ lb (750 g) spreadable cream cheese

½ cup (125 mL) red onion, finely diced

1 cup (250 mL) cilantro, roughly chopped

¼ cup (50 mL) jalapeño, roughly chopped

½ cup (125 mL) shredded cheddar cheese

½ cup (125 mL) shredded Edam cheese

In a food processor, blend all ingredients until well combined. At this point, filling may be stored in an airtight container in the fridge for 1 week.

Evenly distribute filling on tortillas.

>>

Caramelized Onions, Gorgonzola, Yellow Peppers and Fontina Filling

1 recipe Triple Cheese Filling [above]

1½ oz (42 g) Gorgonzola or blue cheese

1½ oz (42 g) grated fontina cheese

Combine Triple Cheese Filling with Gorgonzola or blue cheese and fontina. Mix until well blended. At this point, filling may be stored in an airtight container in the fridge for 1 week.

1 medium yellow bell pepper, roasted and cut into strips

1 recipe Caramelized Onions [see page 169]

Evenly distribute cheese mixture, yellow pepper and onions on the tortillas.

Grilled Chicken, Brie and Artichoke Hearts Filling

2 cups (500 mL) artichoke hearts

¼ cup (50 mL) olive oil

Preheat the oven to 350°F (175°C).

Drain the artichoke hearts and chop them roughly.

Toss with the olive oil and place on a baking sheet. Bake for 10 minutes or until light brown.

Remove from the oven and allow to cool.

4–5 oz (125–150 g) boneless skinless chicken breast

1 recipe Triple Cheese Filling [above]

3½ oz (100 g) brie, cut into chunks

Grill the chicken breast for 6 to 8 minutes per side over medium heat. Cool and cut into thin strips.

Evenly distribute cheese filling over the tortillas.

Top each with strips of chicken, artichoke hearts and brie.

Makes 4 dozen quesadillas

Salsa

from The Lazy Gourmet

⅛ medium red onion, cut into small dice

1 clove garlic, crushed

1 Tbsp (15 mL) chipotle chilies [available in the Mexican section of most grocery stores]

¼ bunch cilantro, chopped

4 cups (1 L) diced tomatoes

1 Tbsp (15 mL) sugar

1 tsp (5 mL) salt

1 tsp (5 mL) lemon juice

Combine all ingredients and process with a hand blender or food processor until the desired consistency is reached.

The sauce will keep for up to a week in the fridge.

Makes 4 cups (1 L)

Chicken Satays with Spicy Peanut Sauce

from *The Lazy Gourmet*

1½ lb (750 g) boneless, skinless chicken breast, cut into twenty-four 2-inch (5-cm) strips

vegetable oil

Soak 24 bamboo skewers in hot water for 5 minutes. Thread chicken strips onto skewers.

Brush chicken with oil. Grill over medium-high heat until cooked, or place the skewers on baking sheets and bake for 10 to 15 minutes at 375°F (190°C).

½ cup (125 mL) Peanut Hoisin Sauce [see page 27]

Place sauce in a dipping bowl. Serve the chicken hot.

Makes 2 dozen skewers

Roasted Garlic on Sicilian Flatbread

from *The Lazy Gourmet*

When the bistro was operating, this was the number one bestseller.

Preheat the oven to 375°F (190°C).

1 bulb garlic

Cut top off garlic bulb to expose cloves. Rub garlic with a bit of olive oil and roast in preheated oven for about 15 minutes. Set aside. Leave oven on.

2 Tbsp (30 mL) butter

1 Tbsp (15 mL) brown sugar

Heat butter and brown sugar together in a saucepan to make a syrup.

1 pear, halved

Cut pear halves into slices without severing the top. Toss pear in syrup and place on a baking sheet. Roast in oven for 10 to 12 minutes. Keep warm.

1 pizza round

2 Tbsp (30 mL) basil oil

Spread basil oil over pizza round and bake at 400°F (200°C) until crispy, about 10 minutes.

Place garlic bulb on the flatbread and fan the pear beside it.

3 oz (75 g) Saint André or other triple-cream brie

Place cheese on top of pear. Return to oven and heat through for another 4 to 5 minutes until cheese starts to melt. Serve straight from the oven.

Serves 2

Toasted Coconut Prawns with Sun-Dried Cherry Chutney

from *The Lazy Gourmet*

Easy to make—and they disappear very quickly!

1½ cups (360mL) flour

6 egg whites

1 tsp (5 mL) salt

1 tsp (5 mL) pepper

In a large mixing bowl, blend flour, egg whites, salt and pepper to make a smooth batter.

24 jumbo prawns, peeled and deveined

1½ cups (360 mL) unsweetened coconut flakes

Dip prawns in batter, then dredge them in coconut.

2 cups (500 mL) vegetable oil

Heat oil in a deep pot to 375°F (190°C).

Deep-fry prawns for 2 minutes. Remove with a slotted spoon and place on paper towel to drain.

Makes 2 dozen prawns

Sun-Dried Cherry Chutney

1 cup (250 mL) sun-dried cherries

½ cup (125 mL) sugar

1 tsp (5 mL) ginger, minced

1 cup (250 mL) water

Combine sun-dried cherries, sugar, ginger and water in a saucepan. Bring to a boil.

Simmer until thick, approximately 15 minutes.

Torta Basilica

from *The Lazy Gourmet*

Slightly altered to make it easier to follow. You'll feel like a hero serving this recipe, which is so easy to make!

½ cup (125 mL) sun-dried tomatoes

1½ cups (360 mL) spreadable cream cheese

Process in food processor and set aside.

½ cup (125 mL) sun-dried tomatoes, cut into julienne

¼ cup (50 mL) pine nuts

½ cup (125 mL) pesto

1½ cups (360 mL) spreadable cream cheese

Use a deep glass bowl and line it with plastic wrap.

Place a small handful of the sun-dried tomatoes on the bottom of the bowl. Spread half of the tomato-cream cheese mixture on top of the tomatoes.

Sprinkle with half of the pine nuts.

Spread half of the pesto over the pine nuts.

Gently spread half of the cream cheese over the pesto.

Sprinkle the rest of the sun-dried tomatoes over the cream cheese.

Spread the rest of the tomato-cream cheese mixture over top.

Spread the last of the pesto over top.

Finish with the last of the cream cheese.

Cover and refrigerate for at least 2 hours.

Turn upside down and remove the plastic wrap.

¼ cup (50 mL) fresh basil

Decorate with fresh basil and remaining half of pine nuts as desired.

Serve with baguette slices or crackers.

Serves 12 to 15

Spanakopita Logs

from *Mama Never Cooked Like This*

This recipe is the only way that I can get my daughter to eat spinach.

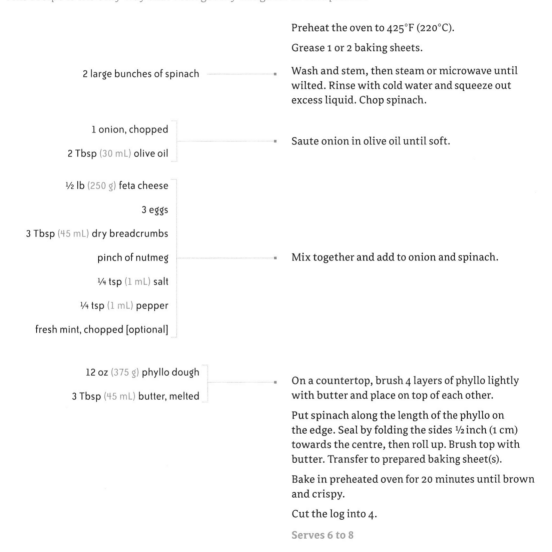

Preheat the oven to 425°F (220°C).

Grease 1 or 2 baking sheets.

2 large bunches of spinach — Wash and stem, then steam or microwave until wilted. Rinse with cold water and squeeze out excess liquid. Chop spinach.

1 onion, chopped
2 Tbsp (30 mL) olive oil — Saute onion in olive oil until soft.

½ lb (250 g) feta cheese
3 eggs
3 Tbsp (45 mL) dry breadcrumbs
pinch of nutmeg — Mix together and add to onion and spinach.
¼ tsp (1 mL) salt
¼ tsp (1 mL) pepper
fresh mint, chopped [optional]

12 oz (375 g) phyllo dough
3 Tbsp (45 mL) butter, melted — On a countertop, brush 4 layers of phyllo lightly with butter and place on top of each other.

Put spinach along the length of the phyllo on the edge. Seal by folding the sides ½ inch (1 cm) towards the centre, then roll up. Brush top with butter. Transfer to prepared baking sheet(s).

Bake in preheated oven for 20 minutes until brown and crispy.

Cut the log into 4.

Serves 6 to 8

Fig Anise Crackers with Saint André Cheese, Mission Figs and Homemade Lemon Jam

Without being conceited, I can honestly say this just might be the best appetizer you've ever had. It was created at The Lazy Gourmet by our resident genius Gina Naples. Thanks, Gina!

Preheat the oven to 350°F (180°C).

3 cups (750 mL) flour
1 tsp (5 mL) baking powder
1 tsp (5 mL) baking soda
1 tsp (5 mL) sugar
½ tsp (2 mL) salt

Sift together.

½ cup (125 mL) butter

Cut butter into dry ingredients until mixture resembles coarse cornmeal.

1½ cups–2 cups (360 mL–500 mL) buttermilk
1 cup (250 mL) black mission figs, chopped fine
1½ Tbsp (22 mL) whole anise seeds, crushed

Add to flour mixture until flour just sticks together. Add a little more buttermilk if necessary.

flour

Turn onto a floured surface and knead briefly. Roll into a log about 2 inches (5 cm) in diameter.

Place on a baking sheet and bake in preheated oven for 20 minutes.

Cool. Reduce heat to 300°F (150°C).

Slice log into ¼-inch (5-mm) slices and lay flat to toast on baking sheet in oven, 12 to 15 minutes until crispy.

Makes 36 crackers

>>

36 pieces Saint André cheese
[about 1 lb (500 g)]

72 pieces black mission figs,
cut into julienne

1 cup (250 mL) Homemade Lemon Jam
[recipe follows]

On each cracker, centre 1 piece of cheese and 2 slices of fig. Drop a small dollop of the lemon jam on top.

Homemade Lemon Jam

3 lemons

Peel lemons and set both peel and fruit aside.

Cut pith off fruit and discard.

¼ cup (50 mL) butter

¼ cup (50 mL) sugar

3 Tbsp (45 mL) lemon juice

Combine lemon and peel with butter, sugar and juice.

Simmer for 8 to 10 minutes.

Purée in blender or food processor.

Chill.

Makes 1 cup (250 mL)

CHAPTER TWO

Soups

Cream of Broccoli Soup

from *Mama Never Cooked Like This*

2–3 lb (1–1.5 kg) broccoli — Steam broccoli for 10 minutes, then drain.

6 Tbsp (90 mL) butter
6 Tbsp (90 mL) flour — Melt butter and add flour, stirring constantly.

2 cups (500 mL) half-and-half
2 cups (500 mL) Vegetable Stock [see recipe page 47]

Add to above and cook until thickened, stirring constantly. Simmer for 5 minutes.

Process half the broccoli in a blender with soup mixture.

Chop remainder of broccoli and add to above.

Makes 6 servings

Gazpacho

from *Mama Never Cooked Like This*

3 cups (750 mL) tomatoes

1½ cups (360 mL) cucumber, peeled

1 green pepper

2 stalks celery

½ cup (125 mL) tomato juice

1 clove garlic, minced — Coarsely chop vegetables.

⅓ cup (75 mL) olive or corn oil

¼ cup (50 mL) red wine vinegar

2 Tbsp (30 mL) parsley

½ tsp (2 mL) salt

½ tsp (2 mL) pepper

Process all ingredients (in order given) in a food processor or blender.

Refrigerate for 6 to 8 hours.

Serve with garlic croutons, chopped green onions, tomatoes, green pepper and cucumber, or top with grated Parmesan cheese.

Makes 8 servings

tip: I sometimes add a little white wine at the end!

Très Simple Chilled Avocado Tomato Soup

from *Mama Never Cooked Like This*

Thanks to Trish Keating for sharing this winning recipe!

2–3 ripe avocados

5 cups (1.25 L) tomato juice

1 small white onion, chopped

1 small green pepper, chopped   • Process well in a blender.

juice of 1 lemon

¼ cup (50 mL) almond paste or crushed almonds

¼ tsp (1 mL) dill weed

3 Tbsp (45 mL) sherry

1 tsp (5 mL) Worcestershire sauce   • Add to above and refrigerate.

2 dashes of Tabasco sauce

salt to taste

pepper to taste

Makes 8 servings

Cold Beet Soup

from *Mama Never Cooked Like This*

My sister Lynn served this to her catering customers recently, to unanimous raves!

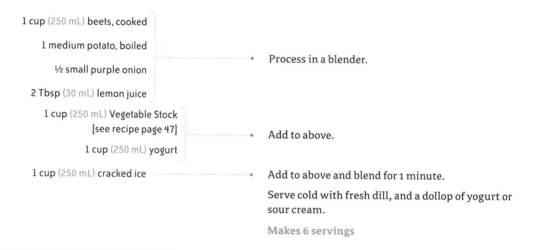

1 cup (250 mL) beets, cooked
1 medium potato, boiled
½ small purple onion
2 Tbsp (30 mL) lemon juice

Process in a blender.

1 cup (250 mL) Vegetable Stock
[see recipe page 47]
1 cup (250 mL) yogurt

Add to above.

1 cup (250 mL) cracked ice

Add to above and blend for 1 minute.

Serve cold with fresh dill, and a dollop of yogurt or sour cream.

Makes 6 servings

Mushroom Soup

from *Mama Never Cooked Like This*

A customer of 27 years made me promise to put this into the new book. Thanks, Roweena!

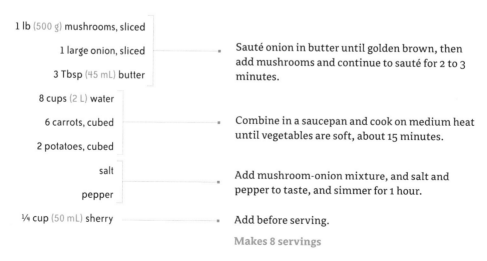

1 lb (500 g) mushrooms, sliced
1 large onion, sliced
3 Tbsp (45 mL) butter

Sauté onion in butter until golden brown, then add mushrooms and continue to sauté for 2 to 3 minutes.

8 cups (2 L) water
6 carrots, cubed
2 potatoes, cubed

Combine in a saucepan and cook on medium heat until vegetables are soft, about 15 minutes.

salt
pepper

Add mushroom-onion mixture, and salt and pepper to taste, and simmer for 1 hour.

¼ cup (50 mL) sherry

Add before serving.

Makes 8 servings

Onion Gratinée

from *Mama Never Cooked Like This*

At the time I created this soup, vegetarian recipes for French onion soup were rare.

2 large onions, sliced thinly

3 Tbsp (45 mL) butter

2 cloves garlic, minced

Sauté onion in butter and garlic until golden brown.

1 Tbsp (15 mL) flour

Add to onions and continue to cook, stirring constantly.

6 cups (1.5 L) Vegetable Stock [see recipe page 47]

1 bay leaf

½ tsp (2 mL) thyme

1 tsp (5 mL) fennel seeds

Add to onion mixture.

Cover and simmer for 40 minutes.

Preheat oven to 500°F (240°C).

10–12 slices French bread, each about 1 inch (2.5 cm) thick

Toast slices in oven, turning until brown on both sides.

Leave oven on.

½ cup (125 mL) port or sherry

Add to soup, just before pouring into ovenproof bowls.

1 cup (250 mL) shredded Swiss Gruyère or Swiss Emmenthal cheese

Float toast on top.

Sprinkle with shredded cheese and bake in oven until cheese melts.

Makes about 6 servings

Minestrone

from *Mama Never Cooked Like This*

I make this soup year-round and vary the vegetables according to the season. It's also a great way to use up leftover vegetables. Just toss them into the soup at the last minute to avoid overcooking. Be creative and have fun with it!

2 small onions, chopped

3–4 stalks celery, chopped

2–3 cups (500–750 mL) zucchini, sliced

1 cup (250 mL) mushrooms, sliced

2 Tbsp (30 mL) olive oil

2 cloves garlic, minced

Sauté onions, celery, zucchini and mushrooms in olive oil and garlic for 3 minutes.

2–3 carrots

½ green pepper, chopped

2 cups (500 mL) fresh tomatoes, chopped or one 14-oz (398-mL) can of tomatoes

2 cups (500 mL) water

1 bay leaf

½ tsp (2 mL) thyme

½ tsp (2 mL) savory

½ tsp (2 mL) marjoram

½ tsp (2 mL) basil

½ tsp (2 mL) rosemary

dash of Tabasco sauce

salt to taste

pepper to taste

Add to above and cook for 5 minutes.

tip: You can add any extra vegetables that you have in your fridge. Rice, noodles or macaroni can also be added.

2 cubes vegetable stock

8 cups (2 L) hot water

Dissolve cubes in hot water.

Add to above and cook for another 20 minutes.

1 cup (250 mL) canned chickpeas

Before serving, add chickpeas and cook for another 2 minutes.

Serve with grated Parmesan cheese.

Makes 8 servings

Wild Mushroom Soup

from *The Lazy Gourmet*

This is my husband Jack's favorite soup. We sometimes leave out the cream entirely and it's still fantastic!

6 cups (1.5 L) mixed wild mushrooms [portobello, shiitake, oyster], sliced

3 shallots, finely chopped

Combine sliced wild mushrooms and chopped shallots, and divide into 4 batches.

2 Tbsp (30 mL) butter

In a large pot with a wide bottom, sauté one batch of mushrooms and shallots in ½ Tbsp (7 mL) of the butter over high heat. When mushrooms start to colour, add another ½ Tbsp (7 mL) of butter and the second batch of mushrooms and shallots. When these are browned, continue with the remaining 2 batches, adding butter and browning the mushrooms lightly. (This technique of cooking the mushrooms in batches is called "layering," as it creates different layers of flavour and texture in one ingredient.)

Remove 1 cup (250 mL) of cooked mushrooms and shallots from the pot and set aside.

8 Tbsp (120 mL) flour

Add flour to the pot of remaining mushrooms; cook and stir over low heat until all the flour is absorbed.

6 cups (1.5 L) chicken or vegetable stock [see Vegetable Stock recipe page 47], heated

Slowly whisk in stock and bring to just a simmer.

1 cup (250 mL) half-and-half

Add half-and-half and return to a simmer. Purée with a hand blender or food processor.

salt and freshly ground white pepper

cayenne

Season to taste with salt, pepper and cayenne. Stir in the reserved mushrooms.

chives, chopped

Ladle into 8 soup bowls and garnish with generous sprinklings of chopped chives.

Makes 8 servings

Roasted Red Pepper Soup

from *The Lazy Gourmet*

Another family favorite soup!

Preheat the oven to 375°F (190°C).

7 cloves garlic

3 medium russet potatoes

Toss garlic in a little olive oil. Place on a baking sheet and roast for about 10 minutes.

While garlic is roasting, peel potatoes and cut into slices about ¼ inch (5 mm) thick.

6 roasted red peppers

8 cups (2 L) Vegetable Stock (see recipe page 47)

salt and freshly ground black pepper

Place peppers, potatoes, garlic and stock into a soup pot. Bring to a boil, then simmer about 20 minutes. Season to taste with salt and pepper.

Purée the soup in a food processor or with a hand blender.

2 Tbsp (30 mL) sherry vinegar

Stir in sherry vinegar to finish.

½ cup (125 mL) fat-free sour cream

Ladle into 8 soup bowls and garnish each with a dollop of fat-free sour cream.

Makes 8 servings

Roasted Tomato and Fennel Soup

from *The Lazy Gourmet*

Preheat the oven to 400°F (200°C).

15 Roma tomatoes, cut in half and seeded

1 cup (250 mL) chopped fresh fennel bulb

3 cloves garlic, peeled

1 onion, peeled and chopped

Combine tomatoes, fennel, garlic cloves and onion in a mixing bowl.

4 Tbsp (60 mL) olive oil

Add olive oil and toss to coat.

Spread vegetables onto 2 rimmed baking sheets and roast in preheated oven for 25 to 30 minutes, turning vegetables at least once, until they are soft and browned.

8 cups (2 L) Vegetable Stock [see recipe page 47]

Combine vegetables and stock in a soup pot. Bring to a boil and simmer slowly for 10 to 15 minutes.

1 Tbsp (15 mL) honey

2 Tbsp (30 mL) balsamic vinegar

Blend honey and balsamic vinegar together and stir into the soup.

Purée the soup with a hand blender or in a food processor.

salt and freshly ground black pepper

Season to taste with salt and pepper.

4 Tbsp (60 mL) extra virgin olive oil [optional]

Ladle into 8 soup bowls, and drizzle ½ Tbsp (7 mL) of olive oil over each bowl.

Makes 8 servings

tip: The fennel adds a slight licorice flavour. Feel free to complete the taste by adding 1–2 tsp (5–10 mL) of Pernod before serving.

Roasted Red Pepper and Tomato Soup

1 Tbsp (15 mL) olive oil

3 red bell peppers, seeded and
cut into quarters

1 large red onion, peeled and sliced

8 cloves garlic, peeled

Coat baking sheet with oil. Place peppers skin side up on baking sheet. Place garlic and onions around peppers. Roast 15 to 20 minutes.

Run peppers under cold water to remove skin. Set aside.

three 14-oz (398-mL) cans of
crushed tomatoes

2 tsp (10 mL) fresh oregano

4 cups (1 L) vegetable or chicken stock
[recipe for Vegetable Stock follows]

Place tomatoes, oregano and stock in large saucepan. Bring to a boil. Reduce heat and simmer for 2 minutes.

Add peppers, onions and garlic. Simmer for 10 minutes.

Transfer to a blender and purée until smooth.

Return to saucepan.

2 Tbsp (30 mL) fresh basil, finely chopped

1 Tbsp (15 mL) granulated sugar

1 tsp (5 mL) sea or kosher salt

freshly ground pepper

Add basil, sugar, salt and pepper to taste. Cook 1 more minute.

3 Tbsp (45 mL) whipping cream

Remove from heat and add the cream.

8 tsp (40 mL) fat-free sour cream

Ladle into 8 soup bowls and garnish each with a dollop of sour cream.

Makes 8 servings

Vegetable Stock

2 medium leeks

2 large onions

6 large carrots, chopped into large chunks

1 yellow or red pepper, seeded and chopped into chunks

1 small bunch celery

1 small bunch parsley

3 bay leaves

1 tsp (5 mL) salt

1 tsp (5 mL) dried thyme [optional]

16 cups (4 L) cold water

Place all ingredients in large pot. Bring to a boil. Reduce and simmer, uncovered, for 1 hour.

Strain in colander. Chill or freeze until ready to use.

Makes 12 cups (3 L)

CHAPTER THREE

Salads

Classic Spinach Salad

from *Mama Never Cooked Like This*

This is a favorite recipe from my first cookbook. I've been told that it *must* be in this book!

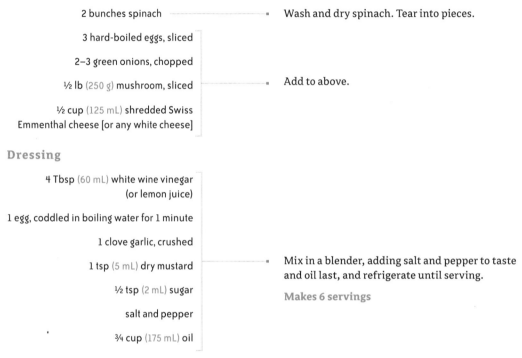

2 bunches spinach — Wash and dry spinach. Tear into pieces.

3 hard-boiled eggs, sliced

2–3 green onions, chopped

½ lb (250 g) mushroom, sliced — Add to above.

½ cup (125 mL) shredded Swiss Emmenthal cheese [or any white cheese]

Dressing

4 Tbsp (60 mL) white wine vinegar (or lemon juice)

1 egg, coddled in boiling water for 1 minute

1 clove garlic, crushed

1 tsp (5 mL) dry mustard — Mix in a blender, adding salt and pepper to taste and oil last, and refrigerate until serving.

½ tsp (2 mL) sugar

salt and pepper

Makes 6 servings

¾ cup (175 mL) oil

variation: You may also want to add the following items to your salad: shrimp, anchovies, olives, apple, beets, grated carrot or toasted almond slivers.

Mimosa Salad

from *Mama Never Cooked Like This*

The "mimosa" refers to the yellow colour of the dressing, which looks wonderful on top of the sliced eggs! This is an old-fashioned recipe that returns to favour periodically.

1 head fancy leaf lettuce — Wash and dry lettuce. Tear into pieces.

3 hard-boiled eggs, sliced

½ lb (250 g) mushrooms, sliced — Lay eggs, mushrooms and parsley over top of lettuce.

1 bunch parsley, chopped fine

Dressing

¾ cup (175 mL) olive oil

¼ cup (50 mL) wine vinegar [white or red]

3 Tbsp (45 mL) lemon juice

¼ tsp (1 mL) dry mustard

¼ tsp (1 mL) cayenne — Mix in a blender.

Makes 4 servings

¼ tsp (1 mL) paprika

¼ tsp (1 mL) turmeric

salt to taste

Mandarin Salad

from *Mama Never Cooked Like This*

This is another classic from *Mama* …. The original recipe was given to me by Mrs. Robinson, the mother of *Mama* …'s publisher, David Robinson.

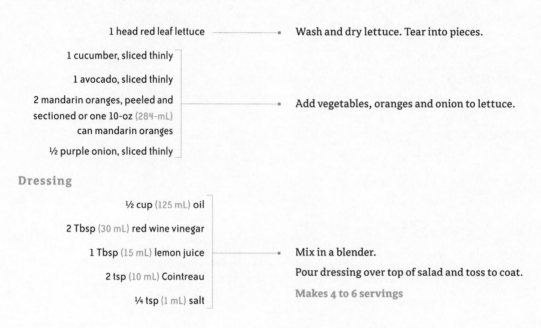

1 head red leaf lettuce — Wash and dry lettuce. Tear into pieces.

1 cucumber, sliced thinly

1 avocado, sliced thinly

2 mandarin oranges, peeled and sectioned or one 10-oz (284-mL) can mandarin oranges — Add vegetables, oranges and onion to lettuce.

½ purple onion, sliced thinly

Dressing

½ cup (125 mL) oil

2 Tbsp (30 mL) red wine vinegar

1 Tbsp (15 mL) lemon juice — Mix in a blender.

2 tsp (10 mL) Cointreau

¼ tsp (1 mL) salt

Pour dressing over top of salad and toss to coat.

Makes 4 to 6 servings

Caesar Salad

from *Mama Never Cooked Like This*

It's a very dramatic salad!

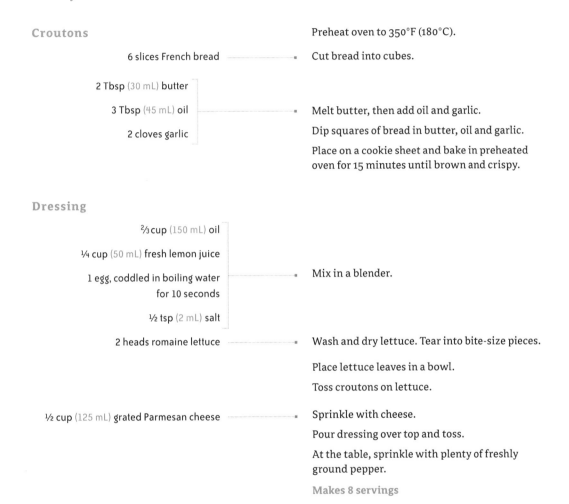

Croutons

Preheat oven to 350°F (180°C).

6 slices French bread — Cut bread into cubes.

2 Tbsp (30 mL) butter
3 Tbsp (45 mL) oil
2 cloves garlic

Melt butter, then add oil and garlic.

Dip squares of bread in butter, oil and garlic.

Place on a cookie sheet and bake in preheated oven for 15 minutes until brown and crispy.

Dressing

⅔ cup (150 mL) oil
¼ cup (50 mL) fresh lemon juice
1 egg, coddled in boiling water for 10 seconds
½ tsp (2 mL) salt

Mix in a blender.

2 heads romaine lettuce — Wash and dry lettuce. Tear into bite-size pieces.

Place lettuce leaves in a bowl.

Toss croutons on lettuce.

½ cup (125 mL) grated Parmesan cheese — Sprinkle with cheese.

Pour dressing over top and toss.

At the table, sprinkle with plenty of freshly ground pepper.

Makes 8 servings

variations: For anchovy lovers, I suggest that you purée 3 Tbsp (45 mL) anchovies in the blender with the dressing. Today, I often replace the lemon juice with balsamic vinegar.

Spicy Orange Marinade for Beets

from Mama Never Cooked Like This

3 lb (1.5 kg) beets

Cook beets in boiling water for 15 to 20 minutes until a fork can be inserted easily. Peel and slice.

Marinade

¾ cup (175 mL) oil

⅓ cup (75 mL) wine vinegar

3 Tbsp (45 mL) orange juice concentrate

1 Tbsp (15 mL) grated fresh ginger [or candied ginger, chopped]

¼ tsp (1 mL) nutmeg

Combine ingredients and pour over beets.

Refrigerate overnight.

Serve on a bed of beet greens and decorate with orange slices.

Makes 6 to 8 servings

tip: For added zip, try adding 1–2 Tbsp (15–30 mL) of Cointreau to the marinade. If the beets you bought have greens intact, don't throw them out—save them for presentation or eat them in a salad.

French Potato Salad

from The Expo 86 Cookbook

A light, fresh salad with a tangy vinaigrette dressing—delicious hot or cold.

14 small new red potatoes, scrubbed

In medium saucepan, boil until just tender (15 to 20 minutes). Drain, cut in halves and let cool 5 minutes.

3 Tbsp (45 mL) chopped fresh parsley

2 Tbsp (30 mL) fresh dill or 2 tsp (10 mL) dried dill

6 Tbsp (90 mL) chopped green onions

4 Tbsp (60 mL) finely chopped red onion

1 large red pepper, chopped [optional]

Combine with potatoes.

>>

⅓ cup (75 mL) red wine vinegar

¾ cup (175 mL) olive oil

2 tsp (10 mL) Dijon mustard

1 clove garlic, crushed

6 turns freshly ground black pepper

Mix well together and toss with potatoes while still warm.

Makes 6 servings

New Potato Salad

from *The Expo 86 Cookbook*

16 small new red potatoes, scrubbed clean

In medium saucepan, boil until just tender (15 to 20 minutes). Drain, cut in halves and let cool 5 minutes.

3 hard-boiled eggs

4 medium green onions, white part and 1 inch (2.5 cm) of green, chopped

4 Tbsp (60 mL) chopped fresh parsley

one 10-oz (284-mL) jar artichoke hearts

Combine in bowl.

Dressing

½ cup (125 mL) sour cream

¾ cup (175 mL) mayonnaise

2 Tbsp (30 mL) Dijon mustard

½ tsp (5 mL) salt

Whisk together, then toss gently with above.

Refrigerate 4 to 6 hours to allow flavours to blend.

Makes 6 to 8 servings

tip: This is best when made with the freshest new potatoes.

Spinach Salad with Peanuts, Apples and Mango Chutney Dressing

from *The Expo 86 Cookbook*

This is a great recipe! The tangy curry-chutney dressing coats the spinach leaves with a glossy shine. My sister Lynn likes to use it for all manner of salads. It's definitely a winner!

1 bunch spinach, washed carefully and dried

1 tart green apple, chopped coarsely

¼ cup (50 mL) chopped green onion

1 cup (250 mL) roasted whole peanuts

Toss together.

Dressing

¼ cup (50 mL) lemon juice

2 Tbsp (30 mL) red wine vinegar

¼ cup (50 mL) mango chutney

1 tsp (5 mL) curry powder

pinch of cayenne

¼ tsp (1 mL) turmeric

½ tsp (2 mL) sugar

½ tsp (2 mL) salt

Combine in blender and blend for 2 minutes.

¾ cup (175 mL) light vegetable oil

Gradually add oil, blending until mixture is smooth.

Toss spinach with dressing and serve immediately.

Makes 4 servings

Curried Chicken Salad

from *The Expo 86 Cookbook*

With this light an entrée, you can treat yourself to a fabulous dessert.

2 cups (500 mL) chopped celery

1 cup (250 mL) seeded and chopped red bell pepper

1 cup (250 mL) seeded and chopped green bell pepper

1 cup (250mL) chopped mushrooms

½ cup (125 mL) coarsely chopped toasted almonds

½ cup (125 mL) halved red seedless grapes

½ cup (125 mL) halved green seedless grapes

½ cup (125 mL) snow peas, lightly steamed

¼ cup (50 mL) chopped fresh parsley

¼ cup (50 mL) chopped red onion

2 cups (500 mL) cooked diced chicken

In large bowl, combine all ingredients.

Dressing

½ cup (125 mL) spreadable cream cheese

½ cup (125 mL) plain yogurt

⅔ cup (150 mL) mayonnaise or low-fat mayonnaise

2 tsp (10 mL) curry powder

2 dashes Tabasco sauce

1 tsp–1 Tbsp (5 mL–15 mL) honey

salt and freshly ground pepper

In separate bowl, whisk together until well blended, using honey and salt and pepper to taste.

Fold dressing into salad. Serve in melon halves (remove seeds) or between croissant halves.

Makes 6 to 8 servings

substitution: Whole chunk tuna can be substituted for chicken.

Marinated New Potato Salad

from *The Expo 86 Cookbook*

Why three potato salads? Because summer is the time for picnics at the beach, with a new twist each time! This salad fits the bill, as the fresh basil makes it unique.

Dressing

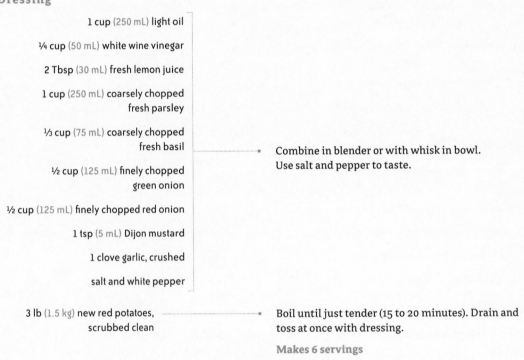

1 cup (250 mL) light oil

¼ cup (50 mL) white wine vinegar

2 Tbsp (30 mL) fresh lemon juice

1 cup (250 mL) coarsely chopped fresh parsley

⅓ cup (75 mL) coarsely chopped fresh basil

½ cup (125 mL) finely chopped green onion

½ cup (125 mL) finely chopped red onion

1 tsp (5 mL) Dijon mustard

1 clove garlic, crushed

salt and white pepper

Combine in blender or with whisk in bowl. Use salt and pepper to taste.

3 lb (1.5 kg) new red potatoes, scrubbed clean

Boil until just tender (15 to 20 minutes). Drain and toss at once with dressing.

Makes 6 servings

Spinach, Portobello and Swiss Cheese Salad with Roasted Garlic Dressing

Preheat oven to 350°F (180°C).

8 portobello mushrooms, stems and gills removed

½ cup (125 mL) balsamic vinegar

2 tsp (10 mL) salt

1 Tbsp (15 mL) black pepper

In a shallow dish, marinate mushrooms with balsamic vinegar, salt and pepper for 10 to 15 minutes.

Place portobellos on a baking sheet and bake for 10 minutes, or until tender. Remove from oven and let cool.

12 cups (3 L) baby spinach

1 cup (250 mL) Roasted Garlic Dressing [recipe follows]

Arrange spinach leaves on a platter and pour garlic dressing over.

Arrange mushrooms (sliced or left whole) around the dish.

1 cup (250 mL) shredded Swiss cheese

Sprinkle Swiss cheese over the spinach. Drizzle with dressing.

Makes 8 servings

Roasted Garlic Dressing

from *The Lazy Gourmet*

Preheat oven to 350°F (180°C).

10 cloves garlic

canola oil

Toss garlic cloves in canola oil. Place in a piece of foil and seal. Roast in preheated oven for 20 to 25 minutes, or until garlic has softened. Allow to cool.

⅓ cup (75 mL) balsamic vinegar

1 Tbsp (15 mL) smooth Dijon mustard

In a bowl, combine roasted garlic, balsamic vinegar and Dijon mustard. Mash until garlic is puréed.

¾ cup (175 mL) olive oil

Slowly whisk in olive oil, until dressing is well blended and smooth.

Makes 1 cup (250 mL)

tip: A blender works well for the dressing. Feel free to take advantage of technology!

Thai Spinach Salad

from *Food to Grow On*

This can be considered a fusion cuisine recipe!

1 large bunch of spinach — Remove stems and wash well. Cut into ribbons.

1 cup (250mL) fresh bean sprouts

½ cup (125 mL) slivered white mushrooms — Toss with spinach.

½ cup (125 mL) slivered toasted almonds

1 red pepper, sliced

Dressing

3 Tbsp (45 mL) lime juice

¼ cup (50 mL) peanut oil

2 Tbsp (30 mL) brown sugar

1 Tbsp (15 mL) minced fresh mint leaves, or mint sauce — Mix together. Pour over the spinach salad.

1 Tbsp (15 mL) minced fresh basil

Makes 4 to 6 servings

1½ tsp (7 mL) minced fresh ginger

½ tsp (2 mL) Chinese chili garlic sauce

pinch of grated nutmeg

Couscous and Chickpea Salad

from Food to Grow On

A meal in itself!

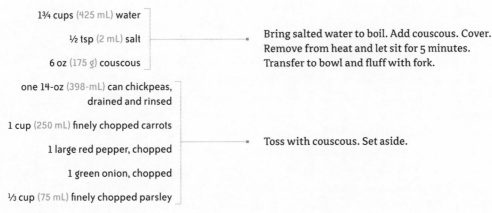

1¾ cups (425 mL) water

½ tsp (2 mL) salt

6 oz (175 g) couscous

Bring salted water to boil. Add couscous. Cover. Remove from heat and let sit for 5 minutes. Transfer to bowl and fluff with fork.

one 14-oz (398-mL) can chickpeas, drained and rinsed

1 cup (250 mL) finely chopped carrots

1 large red pepper, chopped

1 green onion, chopped

⅓ cup (75 mL) finely chopped parsley

Toss with couscous. Set aside.

Dressing

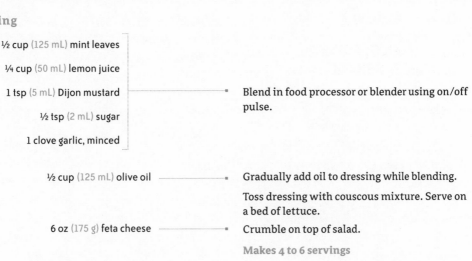

½ cup (125 mL) mint leaves

¼ cup (50 mL) lemon juice

1 tsp (5 mL) Dijon mustard

½ tsp (2 mL) sugar

1 clove garlic, minced

Blend in food processor or blender using on/off pulse.

½ cup (125 mL) olive oil

Gradually add oil to dressing while blending.

Toss dressing with couscous mixture. Serve on a bed of lettuce.

6 oz (175 g) feta cheese

Crumble on top of salad.

Makes 4 to 6 servings

Mira's Favorite Coleslaw

from Food to Grow On

It just gets better with age. This will last several days in the refrigerator until it's time to make more.

Dressing

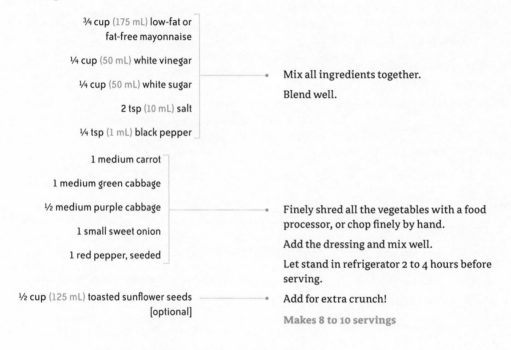

¾ cup (175 mL) low-fat or fat-free mayonnaise

¼ cup (50 mL) white vinegar

¼ cup (50 mL) white sugar

2 tsp (10 mL) salt

¼ tsp (1 mL) black pepper

Mix all ingredients together.

Blend well.

1 medium carrot

1 medium green cabbage

½ medium purple cabbage

1 small sweet onion

1 red pepper, seeded

Finely shred all the vegetables with a food processor, or chop finely by hand.

Add the dressing and mix well.

Let stand in refrigerator 2 to 4 hours before serving.

½ cup (125 mL) toasted sunflower seeds [optional]

Add for extra crunch!

Makes 8 to 10 servings

Strawberry Romaine Spinach Salad with Raspberry Poppy Seed Dressing

from *The Lazy Gourmet*

The demand for this salad surges every summer. It's become a tradition for many family holiday meals.

6 cups (1.5 L) baby spinach

6 cups (1.5 L) romaine lettuce, cut into bite-size pieces

1 pint (500 mL) strawberries, quartered

½ small red onion, cut into ¼-inch (5-mm) slices

Toss spinach, romaine, strawberries and onion together in a large bowl.

1¼ cups (300 mL) Raspberry Poppy Seed Dressing [recipe follows]

Drizzle with the dressing just before serving.

Makes 8 servings

Raspberry Poppy Seed Dressing

½ cup (125 mL) mayonnaise

4 Tbsp (60 mL) raspberry vinegar

¼ cup (50 mL) sugar

¼ cup (50 mL) milk

2 Tbsp (30 mL) poppy seeds

Thoroughly mix all ingredients together with a whisk.

Makes 1¼ cups (300 mL)

Mesclun Greens with Red Pepper, Chèvre and Macadamia Nuts

from *The Lazy Gourmet*

I guarantee that you won't find a better salad dressing anywhere! We also use the sauce for our Hoppa Rolls (see page 24). It makes a fabulous sauce for poached or grilled salmon, too.

12 cups (3 L) mixed greens

1 red bell pepper, cut into ¼-inch (5-mm) slices

Wash greens and put them into a bowl. Toss with pepper.

4 oz (125 g) macadamia nuts, toasted

Coarsely chop the macadamia nuts. Set aside.

6 oz (175 g) chèvre

Gently break chèvre into chunks. Roll into twenty-four 1-inch (2.5-cm) balls.

Roll the balls in the macadamia nuts. Flatten into 1½-inch (4-cm) disks.

Dressing

4 oz (125 g) pickled ginger with juice

3 cloves garlic

1 whole jalapeño pepper, stemmed

one ½-inch (1-cm) piece baby ginger, peeled

1 Tbsp (15 mL) sambal badjak

½ cup (125 mL) rice wine vinegar

1 cup (250 mL) light oil

1 bunch cilantro

For the dressing, put all the remaining ingredients into a blender and process on high until everything is well puréed. Pour one-quarter to one-third of the dressing over the salad. The rest will keep in the fridge for up to 2 weeks.

variation: Warm the chèvre disks for 30 seconds in a 325°F (165°C) oven and gently spoon them onto the salad plates just before serving.

Arrange the salad on 8 serving plates and garnish each plate with 3 macadamia-chèvre disks. For a buffet, gently toss the salad with the chèvre disks.

Makes 8 servings

Sweet Lettuce with Candied Pecans, Pears and Roquefort Dressing

from The Lazy Gourmet

I make this recipe almost every time I have a dinner party, but have never received a complaint! Thanks to Paige Greenberg for sharing the recipe with me. (I recently met Paige's cousin, who gave her the recipe, but I told her that I only give credit to the person who shares a recipe with me!)

1 head butter lettuce

1 small head red leaf lettuce

Wash and dry lettuce, and tear it into bite-size pieces. Place lettuce in a bowl.

4 Tbsp (60 mL) roquefort, Gorgonzola or blue cheese

2 medium Bosc pears, peeled and sliced

Crumble cheese over the lettuce, add pears and gently toss.

Dressing

½ cup (125 mL) light oil

3 Tbsp (45 mL) balsamic vinegar

¼ tsp (1 mL) salt

1 clove garlic, minced

Combine oil, vinegar, salt and garlic. Pour the dressing over the salad.

½ cup (125 mL) Candied Pecans [recipe follows]

Scatter the pecans over top.

Makes 8 to 10 servings

Candied Pecans

½ cup (125 mL) pecans

Heat pecans in a skillet over medium heat until they are hot, about 3 minutes. Toss to prevent burning.

¼ cup (50 mL) sugar

½ tsp (2 mL) freshly ground black pepper

Mix sugar and pepper and toss half the mixture over the pecans.

Reduce heat slightly. Watch the pan and don't do anything until the sugar begins to melt; then toss with a wooden spoon.

Add the rest of the sugar mixture and continue mixing until all the pecans are covered with caramelized sugar.

Pour pecans onto a plate and let cool. Separate the nuts when cooled.

Makes ½ cup (125 mL)

tip: The candied nuts also freeze beautifully.

Tofu Salad

This salad has converted many to tofu who had never ventured near it before. Even better the second day. I love leftovers!

1 lb (500 g) extra-firm tofu

1–2 Tbsp (15–30 mL) canola oil

Cut tofu into 1- × ½-inch (2.5- × 1-cm) strips. Pan-fry tofu until it is golden brown. Place in a container or plate with paper towel to remove excess oil.

½ cup (125 mL) carrots, peeled and sliced

1½ cups (360 mL) napa cabbage or *sui choy*, chopped

½ small red onion, sliced

½ cup (125 mL) snow peas, chopped

1 cup (250 mL) red and/or yellow bell peppers, seeded and chopped

2 bunches green onions, chopped

Combine with the tofu.

Dressing

½ cup (125 mL) black bean sauce

1¼ cups (300 mL) hoisin sauce

¾ Tbsp (10 mL) sambal oelek

¼ cup (50 mL) sesame oil

½ cup (125 mL) vegetable oil

In a bowl, mix black bean sauce, hoisin sauce, sambal oelek and sesame oil together, and slowly pour in vegetable oil until well blended.

Pour 2 cups (500 mL) of the dressing into the salad and mix until everything is nicely coated. Place in a bowl and top with chopped green onion.

Serves 4 as an entrée or 8 as a side salad

Asian Rice Noodle Salad

This is a favorite almost no-fat summer salad. Our herb garden is always overflowing so we make good use of the herbs! I loved developing this recipe at the lake with my friend Paula Brook.

9 oz (300 g) dried vermicelli rice noodles [rice stick] [brown rice if possible]

In a large saucepan, bring some water to a boil.

Add noodles and cook just until tender (2 minutes; 3 to 4 minutes for brown rice noodles).

Lay out noodles on cookie sheets, cover with waxed paper and refrigerate until ready to toss and serve.

Dressing

½ cup (125 mL) lime juice

½ cup (125 mL) Thai sweet chili sauce

2 Tbsp (30 mL) soy sauce

2 Tbsp (30 mL) white sugar

1 tsp (5 mL) sambal badjak

1 tsp (5 mL) ginger syrup [optional]

½ tsp (2 mL) sesame oil

1 cup (250 mL) cilantro leaves

1 cup (250 mL) fresh mint leaves

1 cup (250 mL) Thai basil leaves

Mix all ingredients in blender.

1 red pepper, finely sliced

½ long English cucumber, diced

1 cup (250 mL) tomatoes

Toss vegetables with noodles.

Pour dressing over and serve immediately.

Makes 6 to 8 servings

optional garnish: 1 cup (250 mL) unsalted peanuts, toasted.

tip: If you're going to eat the salad over a two-day stretch, I suggest that you seed the cucumbers before dicing as they create quite a lot of water overnight.

TWO LOW-FAT SALAD DRESSINGS

My husband I went to the Canyon Ranch health spa for a trip, and since then, we have a wonderful salad bar at dinner every evening. There's always a choice of at least two low-fat dressings. These are our favorites, which I developed on our return.

Roasted Pepper and Miso Dressing

Preheat oven to 425°F (220°C).

6 oz (175 g) yellow or red peppers
[2 peppers]

Arrange peppers on baking sheet. Place in preheated oven and let roast until the skin is cracked and dark black.

Remove from oven and place into a paper bag. Let sit for 10 minutes.

Peel the peppers, weigh them, eat excess and add to blender.

3 cloves garlic, crushed

juice of 2 medium limes

1 Tbsp (15 mL) Dijon mustard

1 Tbsp (15 mL) honey

½ cup (125 mL) rice vinegar

4 Tbsp (60 mL) canola oil

Add rest of ingredients to blender and purée.

Makes 1½ cups (360 mL)

1 Tbsp (15 mL) miso [any variety]

¼ cup (50 mL) fresh basil

¼ tsp (1 mL) salt

½ tsp (2 mL) sambal badjak
[optional]

tip: You can make this dressing with lovage instead of basil—if you can find it!

Roquefort Dressing

⅔ cup (150 mL) 1% buttermilk

⅓ cup (150 mL) low-fat mayonnaise

½ cup (125 mL) fat-free sour cream

1 tsp (5 mL) Dijon mustard

3 cloves garlic, crushed — In a large bowl, combine ingredients and whisk.

6 Tbsp (90 mL) balsamic vinegar

1 tsp (5 mL) onion powder

¼ tsp (1 mL) freshly ground black pepper

½ tsp (2 mL) sea or kosher salt

3 oz (75 g) crumbled roquefort cheese or blue cheese — Add cheese and stir to blend.

Makes 1½ cups (360 mL)

CHAPTER FOUR

Side Dishes

Potato Latkes

from *Mama Never Cooked Like This*

5 potatoes	Peel and grate potatoes.
3 eggs, beaten	
1 small onion, grated	
¼ cup (50 mL) flour	Add to above and mix.
salt to taste	
pepper to taste	
oil	Drop by the spoonful into hot oil and fry until golden brown.
	Serve with applesauce or sour cream.

tip: Make tiny ones for unusual hors d'oeuvres.

Makes 6 to 8 servings

Zucchini Pancakes

from *Mama Never Cooked Like This*

A lighter version of the traditional potato latke.

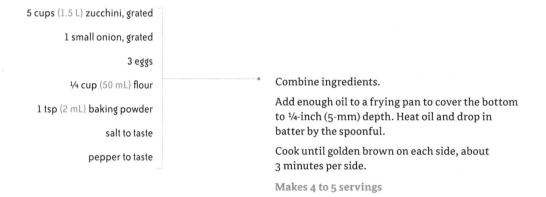

5 cups (1.5 L) zucchini, grated	
1 small onion, grated	
3 eggs	
¼ cup (50 mL) flour	Combine ingredients.
1 tsp (2 mL) baking powder	Add enough oil to a frying pan to cover the bottom to ¼-inch (5-mm) depth. Heat oil and drop in batter by the spoonful.
salt to taste	Cook until golden brown on each side, about 3 minutes per side.
pepper to taste	

Makes 4 to 5 servings

Marinated Cauliflower

from *Mama Never Cooked Like This*

A treat for your friends who are on diets. Stored in an airtight container in the fridge, this marinated cauliflower will last two to three days.

1 head cauliflower ⋯⋯⋯⋯⋯⋯ Cut up cauliflower and steam for 3 minutes, then rinse with cold water to stop the cooking process.

Marinade

⅔ cup (150 mL) red wine vinegar

⅔ cup (150 mL) water

2 tsp (10 mL) parsley
[fresh chopped or dried]

2 tsp (10 mL) dill weed ⋯⋯⋯⋯ Combine ingredients and pour over cauliflower. Refrigerate until cold.

4 cloves garlic

salt to taste

Makes 6 servings

10 peppercorns

Green Beans Provençale

from *Mama Never Cooked Like This*

These are delicious cold the next day.

1½ lb (750 g) green beans — Cut green beans into julienne and steam for 10 minutes, until tender.

Tomato Sauce

1 onion, sliced

2 Tbsp (30 mL) olive oil — Sauté onion in olive oil until translucent.

one 19-oz (540-mL) can tomatoes

one 5½-oz (156-mL) can tomato paste

2 cloves garlic

1 tsp (5 mL) basil

¼ tsp (1 mL) oregano — Add to onion and simmer for 15 minutes.

¼ tsp (1 mL) thyme — Fold into beans.

dash of hot pepper sauce

salt to taste

freshly ground pepper to taste

2–3 Tbsp (30 mL–45 mL) grated Parmesan cheese — Sprinkle with grated Parmesan cheese.

Makes 8 servings

Pommes Anna

from *Mama Never Cooked Like This*

This dish should be golden brown in colour and, if not overcooked, will slice beautifully into pie-shaped servings. The secret is to slice the potatoes very thin! From the school of the French chef Escoffier.

Preheat oven to 400°F (200°C).

Generously brush a 9-inch (2.5-L) soufflé dish with butter.

2 lb (1 kg) potatoes, thinly sliced

¼ cup (50 mL) onion, grated

½ cup (125 mL) butter, melted

salt

pepper

Overlap some potato slices on bottom and around edges of prepared dish.

Sprinkle lightly with grated onion, melted butter, salt and pepper. Place another layer of potato slices into dish, and sprinkle with onion, butter, salt and pepper again.

Repeat until dish is full.

Cover with foil and bake in preheated oven for 30 minutes, then remove foil and bake for another 30 minutes.

Turn over into a heated serving platter.

Makes 6 to 8 servings

Tamari-Ginger Marinated Vegetables

from *The Expo 86 Cookbook*

This salad can marinate overnight. Everyone loves the marinade. Feel free to use it as a salad dressing.

1 cup (250 mL) chopped broccoli [large pieces]

1 cup (250 mL) chopped cauliflower [large pieces]

1 cup (250 mL) snow peas

Blanch in boiling water for 1 minute, then refresh under cold running water until cold.

1 red bell pepper, sliced

½ cup (125 mL) chopped red onion

1 cup (250 mL) small mushroom caps or sliced large mushrooms

¾ cup (175 mL) chopped carrots

Combine with above in a large bowl.

Cover vegetables with Tamari-Ginger Marinade (recipe follows) and let sit at least 1 hour, tossing occasionally.

4 Tbsp (60 mL) sesame seeds, toasted

Sprinkle over salad before serving.

Makes 6 to 8 servings

Tamari-Ginger Marinade

4 Tbsp (60 mL) red wine vinegar

2 Tbsp (30 mL) tamari or soy sauce

1 clove garlic, crushed

2 tsp (10 mL) powdered ginger

1 tsp (5 mL) sugar

In a bowl, combine ingredients in this order.

¾ cup (175 mL) light vegetable oil

2–3 drops sesame oil [optional]

Gradually beat in vegetable oil, adding sesame oil if desired.

Makes 1 cup (250 mL)

Nigiri Rice Triangles

This is another recipe that I learned how to make at a cooking class with Trevor Hopper. I love the combination of sweet, sticky and crispy.

2 cups (500 mL) cooked sticky rice

Form sticky rice into triangles.

Baste with a little oil.

Grill until golden.

Baste with Teriyaki Sauce (recipe follows).

Makes 8 pieces

Teriyaki Sauce

1 cup (250 mL) soy sauce

⅔ cup (150 mL) sake

⅓ cup (75 mL) mirin

⅓ cup (75 mL) sugar

1 Tbsp (15 mL) grated fresh ginger

3 cloves garlic, crushed

1 orange, cut into wedges [leave peel on]

Boil until reduced by 20 percent.

Remove orange pieces.

Makes 2 cups (500 mL)

Lynn's Khao Moak Rice

(Laotian Rice Baked in Banana Leaves)

2 cups (500 mL) Thai fragrant rice	Cook and set aside.
5 kaffir lime leaves	Chop very fine and set aside.
2 green onions	Chop into small pieces and set aside.
¼ cup (60 mL) vegetable oil 1 Tbsp (15 mL) fresh garlic, crushed	Fry together until garlic is brown.
½ tsp (2 mL) red curry paste	Add curry paste and reduce heat. Add some boiling water, about 2 Tbsp (30 mL), to make sauce.
½ cup (125 mL) chopped mushrooms ½ cup (125 mL) chopped red peppers	Add vegetables to sauce and sauté.
2 Tbsp (30 mL) oyster sauce 1 Tbsp (15 mL) soy sauce 2 tsp (10 mL) sugar 1½ tsp (7 mL) lime juice ½ tsp (2 mL) salt 1 tsp (5 mL) curry powder	Add all of these ingredients and mix well. Stir until the sauce is thick.
	Preheat oven to 375°F (190°C).
2–3 banana leaves	Line a 13- × 9-inch (3.5-L) casserole dish with banana leaves.
	Mix sauce together with rice, lime leaves and onion and place in lined casserole. Fold banana leaves over rice so that it is enclosed.
	Bake in preheated oven for 45 minutes.
	Serve with Thai Dipping Sauce (recipe follows).
	Makes 8 servings

tip: The longer you cook the rice in the banana leaf, the sweeter it becomes. I like to serve the casserole on a buffet table and just cut open the top layer of banana leaf with scissors. It's very dramatic.

Thai Dipping Sauce

⅞ cup (200 mL) water
6 Tbsp (90 mL) sugar   ·   Boil until syrup. Let cool.
½ tsp (2 mL) salt

5 cloves garlic   ·   Grind garlic and chili together and add to syrup.
3 fresh chilies

1 Tbsp (15 mL) chili sauce
4 Tbsp (60 mL) fish sauce   ·   Add and mix well.
6 Tbsp (100 mL) fresh lime juice

1 oz (25 g) fresh coriander   ·   Sprinkle with coriander.

Makes 2 cups (500 mL)

Mixed Wild Rices and Wild Mushrooms

This is our new family favorite side dish! Another recipe developed at The Lazy Gourmet.

1 large onion, chopped

2 Tbsp (30 mL) olive oil

2 cloves garlic, crushed

In a medium saucepan, sauté onion and garlic in oil and cook until transparent.

2 cups (500 mL) mixed wild rices

Add rices and cook until well coated, about 1 minute.

6 cups (1.5 L) vegetable broth

Add broth; stir until blended.

Cover immediately and bring to a boil. Reduce heat to low and simmer until all of the liquid is absorbed (about 40 minutes).

Do not stir during cooking process!

3 cups (750 mL) assorted mushrooms, sliced

1 Tbsp (15 mL) butter

2 cloves garlic, crushed

In large saucepan, sauté until mushrooms are tender.

Mix into cooked rices.

¾ cup (175 mL) chopped pecans, toasted

Toss into rices, reserving some to decorate platter when serving.

Makes 8 servings

Uncle Peter's Fried Rice

Developed at the lake on a warm summer's night. Uncle Peter has celiac disease and cannot eat wheat or gluten, so we had to find a sauce that would be something like oyster sauce and soy. Now we just eat this fried rice.

2 Tbsp (30 mL) oil	
½ large onion, chopped	Fry onion until crispy. Add garlic and cook until soft.
2–3 cloves garlic	
1 egg	Add and cook by scrambling with above.
3–4 cups (750 mL–1 L) leftover rice [brown or white]	Add rice and toss.

Sauce

2 Tbsp (30 mL) Thai sweet chili sauce	
2 Tbsp (30 mL) ketchup	
2 Tbsp (30 mL) fish sauce	Mix sauce ingredients. Pour over rice and cook until heated.
1 Tbsp (15 mL) wheat-free soy sauce	
3 drops sesame oil	

Makes 4 to 6 servings

Lynn's Green Beans or Broccoli with Nami Sauce

This has a very rich flavour and makes you want to eat your greens!

2 lb (1 kg) green beans or broccoli florets .... • Steam or boil or microwave until tender.

Nami Sauce

4 Tbsp (60 mL) soy sauce

4 Tbsp (60 mL) mirin [sweet rice wine]

2 Tbsp (30 mL) rice vinegar

⅓ cup (75 mL) Japanese roasted sesame
sauce [tahini will work if you
can't find the Japanese product] .... • Blend well with whisk.

Pour sauce over vegetables.

2 tsp (10 mL) sugar

2 Tbsp (30 mL) roasted sesame seeds

2 Tbsp (30 mL) roasted sesame seeds
[optional] .... • Sprinkle on top for presentation if desired.

Makes 8 to 10 servings

Aida's Yams with Marmalade Glaze

This recipe is as easy as it appears and is always a hit, served with chicken or fish.

Preheat oven to 400°F (200°C).

Grease a 13- × 9-inch (3.5-L) casserole dish.

4 large yams or sweet potatoes — Wash yams and prick with a fork. Wrap tightly with foil.

Bake in preheated oven for 1 hour.

Reduce heat to 350°F (180°C).

Let cool. Remove foil. With paring knife, gently remove outer skin.

Slice into 1½-inch (4-cm) thick slices and lay out in prepared casserole dish.

½ cup (125 mL) marmalade, your choice [I like lemon and pear]

¼ cup (50 mL) orange juice — Mix together and brush or spoon gently over yams.

Bake 18 to 20 minutes until hot and marmalade sizzles.

Makes 8 to 10 servings

Squash Brulé

A terrific way to eat squash. Try it with both types of squash at once. Thanks to Rena for the recipe, which we have at least once a week!

Preheat oven to 350°F (180°C).

Grease a 9-inch (23-cm) deep-dish ceramic pie plate.

2 lb (1 kg) acorn or butternut squash — Peel and cut squash into large chunks.

10 cups (2.5 L) water — Boil squash in water for 10 minutes.

1 egg
½ cup (125 mL) half-and-half — Mash squash and mix with egg, half-and-half and nutmeg. Pour into dish.
½ tsp (2 mL) nutmeg

1 Tbsp (15 mL) butter — Dot with butter.

Bake in preheated oven for 20 minutes.

2 Tbsp (30 mL) brown sugar — Press sugar through a sieve. Sprinkle lightly over the squash.

Put squash under broiler for 2 minutes until golden.

Makes 6 to 8 servings

Spinach Mushroom Gratin

I often vary the cheese and the toppings. I like to serve this with fish, but it works well with everything, especially lamb or beef.

Preheat oven to 375°F (190°C).

Grease a 13- × 9-inch (3.5-L) casserole dish.

2 lb (1 kg) spinach leaves [please weigh]	Rinse spinach, and steam or microwave until wilted. Drain well and squeeze out excess liquid; set aside.
2 Tbsp (30 mL) butter	In saucepan, melt butter.
2 leeks, sliced thin [white and light green parts only]	Sauté leeks until soft.
2 cloves garlic, crushed	Add garlic and cook 1 minute.
6 oz (175 g) mushrooms, sliced	Add mushrooms and cook until just softened. Put mixture into prepared casserole dish.
1 cup (250 mL) grated Parmesan [Reggiano or Grana Padano]	Sprinkle over mixture.
1 whole egg 2 egg whites ½ cup (125 mL) milk	Put eggs, milk and cooled spinach into food processor or blender. Process well. Pour into casserole dish and use a fork to incorporate everything (smush around).

Topping

¼ cup (50 mL) grated Parmesan [Reggiano or Grana Padano] ⅓ cup (75 mL) crushed pecans ¼ cup (50 mL) breadcrumbs	Mix together cheese, pecans and breadcrumbs and sprinkle over spinach mixture. Bake in preheated oven for 25 to 30 minutes.

Makes 10 to 12 servings

CHAPTER FIVE

Family Traditions

Chocolate Orange Passover Cake

This recipe was given to me by Jeannie Watchuk, who started out a customer, became a good friend, then a judge and once even worked at The Lazy Gourmet. Any leftovers are frequently devoured at breakfast after the first Seder!

Preheat the oven to 350°F (180°C).

Lightly grease a 9- or 10-inch (3- or 4-L) tube pan with oil, and flour with matzo cake meal.

9 egg whites — Beat until foamy.

½ cup (125 mL) sugar — Slowly add to egg whites, beating until stiff.

9 egg yolks
½ cup (125 mL) sugar
— Beat together, then fold into whites.

1 cup (250 mL) ground almonds
½ cup (125 mL) chopped almonds [or walnuts]
1 Tbsp (15 mL) potato starch
3 Tbsp (45 mL) sifted matzo cake meal — Combine, then gently fold into egg mixture.

1 Tbsp (15 mL) powdered instant coffee

4 oz (125 g) semi-sweet chocolate, coarsely grated

grated rind of 1 large orange

Pour batter into prepared pan. Bake in preheated oven for 45 minutes.

When cool, cover with Chocolate Honey Glaze (recipe follows).

Makes 10 servings

Chocolate Honey Glaze

6 oz (175 g) semi-sweet chocolate, chopped

¼ cup (50 mL) unsalted butter — Melt together, stirring until smooth.

2–3 Tbsp (30–45 mL) honey

Pour over cooled cake.

Makes 1 cup (250 mL)

Rugelah, Rogelach or Kuffels

Whatever the name, they're delicious!

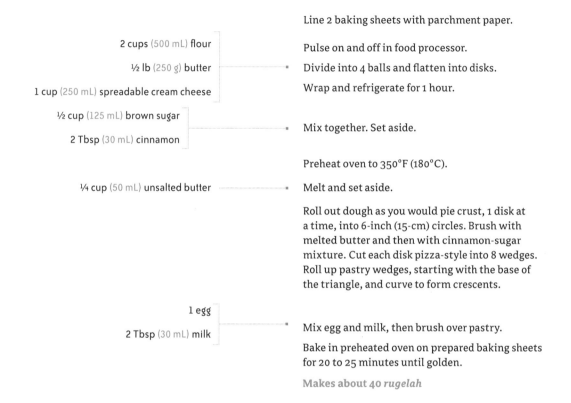

2 cups (500 mL) flour
½ lb (250 g) butter
1 cup (250 mL) spreadable cream cheese

Line 2 baking sheets with parchment paper.

Pulse on and off in food processor.
Divide into 4 balls and flatten into disks.
Wrap and refrigerate for 1 hour.

½ cup (125 mL) brown sugar
2 Tbsp (30 mL) cinnamon

Mix together. Set aside.

Preheat oven to 350°F (180°C).

¼ cup (50 mL) unsalted butter

Melt and set aside.

Roll out dough as you would pie crust, 1 disk at a time, into 6-inch (15-cm) circles. Brush with melted butter and then with cinnamon-sugar mixture. Cut each disk pizza-style into 8 wedges. Roll up pastry wedges, starting with the base of the triangle, and curve to form crescents.

1 egg
2 Tbsp (30 mL) milk

Mix egg and milk, then brush over pastry.

Bake in preheated oven on prepared baking sheets for 20 to 25 minutes until golden.

Makes about 40 *rugelah*

Apple Pecan Kugel

I developed this recipe from a memory of a delicious kugel that our late cousin Carol Gitelman used to make for our family. I recommend it for Rosh Hashanah, the Jewish New Year, but it's a favorite year-round for B'nai Mitzvah customers. We're now making individual kugels in muffin tins.

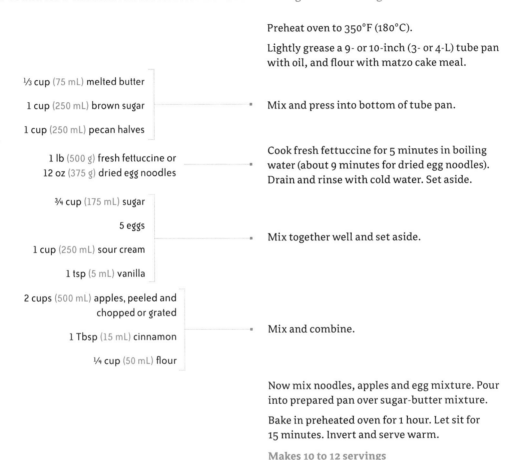

Preheat oven to 350°F (180°C).

Lightly grease a 9- or 10-inch (3- or 4-L) tube pan with oil, and flour with matzo cake meal.

⅓ cup (75 mL) melted butter
1 cup (250 mL) brown sugar
1 cup (250 mL) pecan halves

Mix and press into bottom of tube pan.

1 lb (500 g) fresh fettuccine or
12 oz (375 g) dried egg noodles

Cook fresh fettuccine for 5 minutes in boiling water (about 9 minutes for dried egg noodles). Drain and rinse with cold water. Set aside.

¾ cup (175 mL) sugar
5 eggs
1 cup (250 mL) sour cream
1 tsp (5 mL) vanilla

Mix together well and set aside.

2 cups (500 mL) apples, peeled and chopped or grated
1 Tbsp (15 mL) cinnamon
¼ cup (50 mL) flour

Mix and combine.

Now mix noodles, apples and egg mixture. Pour into prepared pan over sugar-butter mixture.

Bake in preheated oven for 1 hour. Let sit for 15 minutes. Invert and serve warm.

Makes 10 to 12 servings

Pearl's Sponge Cake

This recipe was given to me by my mother's dear friend Pearl Kafetz. It's my customers' favorite Passover sponge cake. It's great for breakfast with fresh berries.

Preheat oven to 325°F (160°C).

⅛ cup (30 mL) cocoa

¼ cup (60 mL) sugar

¼ cup (60 mL) boiling water

Mix together and set aside.

1 cup (250 mL) matzoh meal

¼ cup (60 mL) potato starch

pinch salt

¾ cups (175 mL) sugar

Mix dry ingredients together. Set aside.

10 egg whites

¾ cup (175 mL) sugar

Beat egg whites until stiff. Gradually add sugar. Beat until glossy.

10 egg yolks

½ cup (125 mL) canola oil

½ cup (125 mL) orange juice

Whisk together yolks, oil and juice.

Then fold into whites

Gently fold in dry ingredients from above.

Fill prepared angel food pan with ¾ of the batter.

Mix cocoa mixture into rest of batter and swirl it into the angel pan with the rest of the cake to create a marble effect.

Bake at 325°F (160°C) for about one hour or until set.

Makes 12 servings

Passover Schmoo Torte

This is a Winnipeg recipe that is also a year-round favorite. I have no idea where the name "Schmoo" came from, but mention it to a Jewish person from Winnipeg and watch their eyes light up! The recipe was given to me by Barbara Halparin, who married a Winnipegger!

Preheat oven to 350°F (180°C).

Torte

12 egg yolks
¾ cup (175 mL) sugar
1½ Tbsp (22 mL) lemon juice

Beat together until light.

2 cups (500 mL) pecans, finely ground
⅓ cup (75 mL) matzo cake meal

Mix together and add to yolk mixture.

12 egg whites

Beat until soft peaks form.

pinch of salt
1 cup (250 mL) sugar

Slowly add to egg whites, beating to stiff peaks, then fold into yolk mixture.

Place in ungreased tube pan. Bake in preheated oven 55 to 60 minutes. Invert to cool before removing from pan.

Filling

2 cups (500 mL) whipping cream
3 Tbsp (45 mL) icing sugar [optional]
1 tsp (5 mL) vanilla

Beat together until soft peaks form.

Slice cake into 5 layers. Spread each layer with whipped cream filling, leaving enough to cover top and sides of cake.

Makes 12 servings

Caramel Sauce

1 cup (250 mL) brown sugar
1 cup (250 mL) whipping cream
¼ cup (50 mL) unsalted butter

Mix together and bring to a boil. Boil for 6 to 7 minutes. Remove from heat.

Drizzle room-temperature sauce over cake and serve the rest on the side.

Makes about 2 cups (500 mL)

Miriam's Gefilte Fish Loaf

My late mother-in-law, Miriam Glassman Lutsky, gave me this recipe and it's been the Lazy Gourmet gefilte fish ever since! Gefilte fish is traditionally boiled, which leaves your kitchen smelling like Passover for months to come. I prefer this version.

3 lb (1.5 kg) mixed fish [such as
1½ lb (750 g) white fish,
1 lb (500 g) pickerel and
½ lb (250 g) salmon], ground

3 eggs

1 cup (250 mL) cold water

⅓ cup (75 mL) matzo meal

1 small onion, grated

1 carrot, grated or chopped
[about 1 cup (250 mL)]

4 tsp (20 mL) salt

1 tsp (5 mL) pepper

1 Tbsp (15 mL) granulated sugar

Preheat the oven to 350°F (180°C).

Line a 9- × 5-inch (2-L) loaf pan with parchment paper.

Place fish in large bowl. Add eggs, water, matzo meal, onion, carrot, salt, pepper and sugar.

Gently combine ingredients.

Place mixture in prepared pan. Cover with foil.

Place a roasting pan in preheated oven and half fill the pan with hot or boiling water. Gently place pan of fish in water bath.

Bake for 1 hour. Uncover pan and bake 30 minutes longer.

Cool fish and then refrigerate for a few hours or overnight. Remove from pan and slice. Serve with horseradish.

Makes 8 to 10 servings

Aunt Naomi's Buttermilk Kugel

My Aunt Naomi shared this recipe with the family. She's from Winnipeg, which guarantees that it's delicious! Serve with fresh berries and yogurt or light sour cream. Perfect for Sunday brunch.

Preheat the oven to 350°F (180°C).

Butter a 13- × 9-inch (3.5-L) Pyrex dish.

1 lb (500 g) dry egg noodles — Cook according to package instructions.

4 eggs

½ cup (125 mL) sugar

½ cup (125 mL) butter, melted

4 cups (1 L) buttermilk

Mix together and add noodles.

Place into prepared Pyrex dish. Pour buttermilk over noodles.

Bake in preheated oven for 35 minutes.

1½ cups (360 mL) corn flakes

½ cup (125 mL) brown sugar

2 Tbsp (30 mL) melted butter

Place flakes in plastic bag and roll over with a rolling pin. Mix with brown sugar and melted butter. Spoon over top of noodles.

Reduce heat to 325°F (160°C) and bake an additional 30 minutes.

Makes 12 servings

Rosh Hashanah Honey Cake

For 25 years, customers have been begging me for this recipe. I'm finally ready to part with it. Enjoy!

Preheat oven to 325°F (160°C).

Lightly grease a 9- or 10-inch (3- or 4-L) tube pan with oil, and flour with matzo cake meal.

4 eggs
1½ cups (375 mL) sugar
1 cup (250 mL) oil
1 cup (250 mL) honey

Beat together.

1 cup (250 mL) tea [strong]
juice of ½ lemon

Mix and add to above.

2½ cups (625 mL) flour
1 tsp (5 mL) baking soda
2 tsp (10 mL) baking powder
1 tsp (5 mL) cinnamon
½ tsp (2 mL) allspice
¼ tsp (1 mL) cloves
¼ tsp (1 mL) ginger

Sift together and add to above. Mix to combine (batter will be thin). Pour into prepared pan.

Bake in preheated oven for approximately 1 hour and 15 minutes.

Makes 10 to 12 servings

Sherry's Matzo Toffee

Cousin Sherry shared this recipe and it brings new meaning to matzo!

Preheat oven to 350°F (180°C).

vegetable oil spray — Line a large baking sheet with foil; spray foil generously with oil spray.

6 squares matzo — Line prepared baking sheet with matzo.

1 cup (250 mL) butter
1 cup (250 mL) brown sugar — Melt butter and brown sugar in a saucepan and boil 3 minutes while stirring. Pour over matzo.

Put baking sheet in preheated oven for 5 minutes until topping bubbles. Remove from oven.

12 oz (375 g) chocolate chips or semi-sweet chocolate, chopped
1 cup (250 mL) sliced or slivered almonds, toasted until golden brown — Sprinkle chocolate pieces over hot toffee immediately. Chocolate will melt within 2 minutes. Spread liquefied chocolate evenly over toffee and sprinkle with toasted nuts.

Cool in fridge and break into pieces. Can be frozen and then easily broken into pieces.

Makes 1½ lb (750 g)

Lynn's Hot Fudge Sauce

Believe it or not, this recipe was first given to Lynn by our sister Rena, who is a nutritionist. I assumed that she did not want her name associated with it!

1½ cups (375 mL) semi-sweet chocolate chips
½ cup (125 mL) butter
¾ cup (175 mL) evaporated milk — Melt together.

2 cups (500 mL) icing sugar — Add to chocolate mixture. Stir in until smooth.

Simmer for 8 to 10 minutes.

Makes 3 cups (750 mL)

Wild Mushroom Risotto Balls   p. 17

Lynn's Khao Moak Rice **p. 78**

Sablefish with Lime Ginger Sauce   p. 120

Quinoa Pine Nut Pilaf   p. 110

Mocha Mousse Meringue Cake   p. 98

Cranberry Lazy Gourmet Bars for Christmas

Looks beautiful on a platter of Christmas baking. This is our special Lazy Gourmet Christmas bar.

Grease and flour a 9-inch (2.5-L) square baking pan.

Layer One

½ cup (125 mL) butter

¼ cup (50 mL) sugar

1 egg

1 tsp (10 mL) vanilla extract

> Mix together and set over boiling water.
> Stir until thickened.

2 cups (500 mL) vanilla wafer crumbs

1 cup (250 mL) coconut

½ cup (125 mL) chopped nuts [optional]

> Combine with above and press into prepared pan.

Layer Two

¼ cup (50 mL) butter, softened

2 Tbsp (30 mL) milk

2½ cups (625 mL) icing sugar

1½ Tbsp (22 mL) cranberry sauce

2 Tbsp (30 mL) dried cranberries

> Mix well and spread over Layer One.

Layer Three

6 oz (175 g) white chocolate

> Melt over hot water and spread gently over Layer Two. Chill until just set.
>
> Cut into squares and have a blast!
>
> **Makes 16 squares**

Mocha Mousse Meringue Cake

It's a little time-consuming, but easy and fun to make, with a big payoff! You'll wow your guests and family. Perfect for Passover or when guests have wheat or gluten allergies.

Preheat oven to 250°F (120°C).

Line 2 baking sheets with waxed or parchment paper.

icing sugar · Lightly sift icing sugar over paper. Trace four 8-inch (20-cm) circles on baking sheets (a standard salad plate can be used as a guide).

Meringue

4 Tbsp (60 mL) instant coffee

2 tsp (10 mL) hot water · · · · · · · · · · · · · · · Dissolve coffee in water. Set aside.

2 cups (500 mL) icing sugar

6 Tbsp (90 mL) cocoa powder · · · · · · · · · Sift together and set aside.

10 egg whites · In large bowl, beat until soft peaks form.

1½ cups (360 mL) sugar · · · · · · · · · · · · · · · Add to egg whites 1 Tbsp (15 mL) at a time. Continue beating until stiff peaks form.

Beat in coffee mixture.

Fold in cocoa mixture.

Make 4 meringue disks, using 1¼ cups (300 mL) of mixture for each, on the paper-lined baking sheets, following circles traced earlier.

Line another baking sheet with waxed or parchment paper. Put extra meringue mixture into piping bag and pipe onto sheet in long tubes.

Bake until crisp (approximately 1 hour).

Cut meringue tubes on sheet into 3-inch (8-cm) pieces once they are cool.

\>>

Mousse

8 oz (250 g) semi-sweet chocolate
4 oz (125 g) bitter chocolate
1½ cups (375 mL) unsalted butter
¼ cup (50 mL) corn syrup

Melt over hot water. Stir until smooth. Let cool.

2 tsp (10 mL) vanilla extract

Add to chocolate mixture. Set mixture aside.

⅔ cup (150 mL) sugar
4 Tbsp (60 mL) water

In small saucepan, stir over low heat until sugar is dissolved. Boil 1 minute.

8 egg whites

Beat until soft peaks form.

Gradually, over a period of 5 minutes, beat in boiling syrup and continue to beat until cool.

Fold half of egg white mixture into chocolate. When incorporated, fold in remainder.

1 cup (250 mL) whipping cream

Beat until soft peaks form. Fold into chocolate mixture.

Refrigerate until just beginning to set.

Put dollop of mousse in centre of platter to keep meringue from sliding. Divide remainder into 5 portions.

Place meringue disk on platter.

Top with 1 portion of mousse.

Continue to layer meringue and mousse.

Spread remaining mousse around sides.

Press tubes of meringue around edges of cake side by each.

Chop up remaining pieces and toss on top of cake.

Dust with cocoa or icing sugar.

Makes 12 servings

Fruitarian Mincemeat

from Mama Never Cooked Like This

Mincemeat is traditionally made with suet. The Lazy Gourmet invented this recipe so that suet would not be necessary.

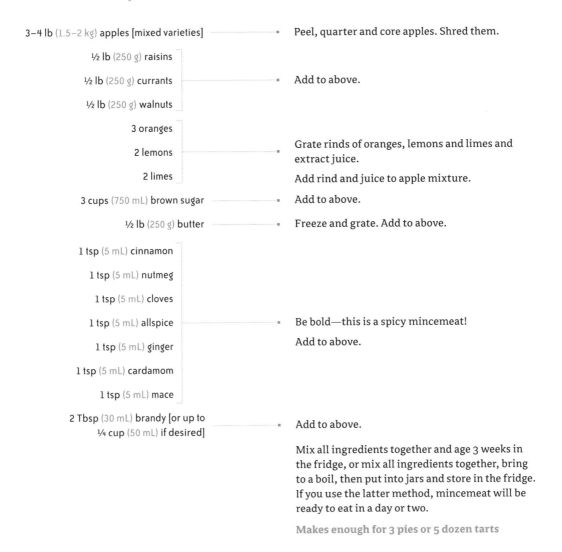

3–4 lb (1.5–2 kg) apples [mixed varieties]	Peel, quarter and core apples. Shred them.
½ lb (250 g) raisins	
½ lb (250 g) currants	Add to above.
½ lb (250 g) walnuts	
3 oranges	Grate rinds of oranges, lemons and limes and extract juice.
2 lemons	
2 limes	Add rind and juice to apple mixture.
3 cups (750 mL) brown sugar	Add to above.
½ lb (250 g) butter	Freeze and grate. Add to above.
1 tsp (5 mL) cinnamon	
1 tsp (5 mL) nutmeg	
1 tsp (5 mL) cloves	
1 tsp (5 mL) allspice	Be bold—this is a spicy mincemeat!
1 tsp (5 mL) ginger	Add to above.
1 tsp (5 mL) cardamom	
1 tsp (5 mL) mace	
2 Tbsp (30 mL) brandy [or up to ¼ cup (50 mL) if desired]	Add to above.

Mix all ingredients together and age 3 weeks in the fridge, or mix all ingredients together, bring to a boil, then put into jars and store in the fridge. If you use the latter method, mincemeat will be ready to eat in a day or two.

Makes enough for 3 pies or 5 dozen tarts

Carrot *and* Sweet Potato Tzimmes

from Mama Never Cooked Like This

This carrot and sweet potato tzimmes is traditionally served for Rosh Hashanah, the Jewish New Year, to ensure a "sweet year." We serve it for Passover as well.

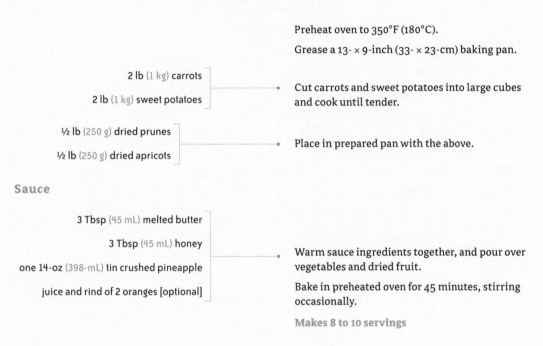

Preheat oven to 350°F (180°C).

Grease a 13- × 9-inch (33- × 23-cm) baking pan.

2 lb (1 kg) carrots

2 lb (1 kg) sweet potatoes

Cut carrots and sweet potatoes into large cubes and cook until tender.

½ lb (250 g) dried prunes

½ lb (250 g) dried apricots

Place in prepared pan with the above.

Sauce

3 Tbsp (45 mL) melted butter

3 Tbsp (45 mL) honey

one 14-oz (398-mL) tin crushed pineapple

juice and rind of 2 oranges [optional]

Warm sauce ingredients together, and pour over vegetables and dried fruit.

Bake in preheated oven for 45 minutes, stirring occasionally.

Makes 8 to 10 servings

Grandma Faye's Cheese Blintz Logs

This recipe has been a B'nai Mitzvah special for over 25 years at The Lazy Gourmet. Customers have been begging me for the recipe for many years. Here it is at last!

Preheat the oven to 350°F (180°C).

Pastry

1 cup (250 mL) butter

2 cups (500 mL) flour

Combine flour and butter until crumbly.

1 egg yolk

½ cup (125 mL) sour cream

1 tsp (5 mL) baking powder

Add to flour mixture and mix together.

Divide into 3 logs. Refrigerate for 2 to 3 hours.

Filling

1½ lb (750 g) pressed cottage cheese

3 eggs

6 Tbsp (90 mL) sugar

Blend together.

Egg Wash

1 egg

2 Tbsp (30 mL) water

Mix together.

Roll out each pastry log into rectangle. Brush egg wash over edges.

Spread one-third of filling in centre of each, and fold ends to seal.

1 Tbsp (15 mL) berry sugar [optional]

Brush top with egg wash and sprinkle with sugar if desired.

Bake in preheated oven for 20 to 25 minutes until golden brown.

Serve with fresh berries and sour cream.

Makes 3 logs (6 servings)

The Lazy Gourmet Christmas Brandy Cake

The Lazy Gourmet was asked to make this cake—a recipe of Emily Dickinson's—to be served at the production of a play about Dickinson performed at the Waterfront Theatre by the wonderful Claire Coulter. It then became the Lazy Gourmet Christmas cake.

Preheat the oven to 325°F (160°C).

Grease and flour a 13- × 9-inch (33- × 23-cm) baking pan.

1 cup (250 mL) butter
1¾ cup (425 mL) white sugar

Cream until light.

4 eggs

Add 1 at a time.

¾ cup (175 mL) dark molasses

Add and mix.

1¾ cup (425 mL) flour
½ tsp (2 mL) nutmeg
1½ tsp (7 mL) cloves
1½ tsp (7 mL) mace
1½ tsp (7 mL) cinnamon
½ tsp (2 mL) ginger
½ tsp (2 mL) baking soda
¼ tsp (1 mL) salt

Sift together.

⅓ cup (75 mL) brandy

Add dry ingredients alternately with brandy to wet mixture above.

½ lb (250 g) sultana raisins
¾ cup (175 mL) grated candied ginger

Stir into above.

Pour into prepared pan. Bake in preheated oven for 45 minutes until toothpick inserted in centre comes out clean. Cool to room temperature.

Icing

¾ cup (175 mL) icing sugar
2 Tbsp (30 mL) brandy
2 Tbsp (30 mL) whipping cream

Mix together. Add icing sugar until icing is smooth but pourable.

Spread over cooled cake.

Makes 24 squares

Reva's Passover Rolls

When you haven't had bread for a while, these really hit the spot! I serve them with gefilte fish for the first course of the Seder meal.

Preheat the oven to 350°F (180°C).

Grease a baking sheet thoroughly.

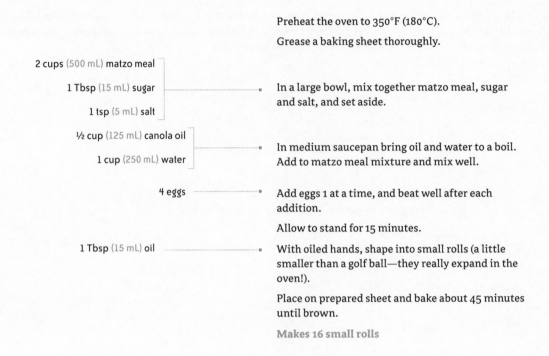

2 cups (500 mL) matzo meal
1 Tbsp (15 mL) sugar
1 tsp (5 mL) salt

In a large bowl, mix together matzo meal, sugar and salt, and set aside.

½ cup (125 mL) canola oil
1 cup (250 mL) water

In medium saucepan bring oil and water to a boil. Add to matzo meal mixture and mix well.

4 eggs

Add eggs 1 at a time, and beat well after each addition.

Allow to stand for 15 minutes.

1 Tbsp (15 mL) oil

With oiled hands, shape into small rolls (a little smaller than a golf ball—they really expand in the oven!).

Place on prepared sheet and bake about 45 minutes until brown.

Makes 16 small rolls

Vanilla Macaroons for Passover

from *The Lazy Gourmet*

Another family favorite year-round and great for those with wheat and gluten allergies.

Preheat the oven to 325°F (160°C).

Line a baking sheet with parchment paper.

¾ cup (175 mL) white sugar
2½ cups (625 mL) long-thread coconut
2 large egg whites
1 tsp (5 mL) vanilla extract
¼ tsp (1 mL) salt

Combine until well blended.

Drop by spoonfuls onto prepared sheet. (They can also be shaped into pyramid shapes.)

Bake 12 to 15 minutes until lightly browned.

Allow to cool before removing from parchment.

Makes 12 to 14 macaroons

Chocolate Macaroons for Passover

from *The Lazy Gourmet*

These macaroons are ideal for any occasion, but were designed specifically for Passover. It's fun to try to make the pyramid shape, to bring extra resonance to holiday celebrations!

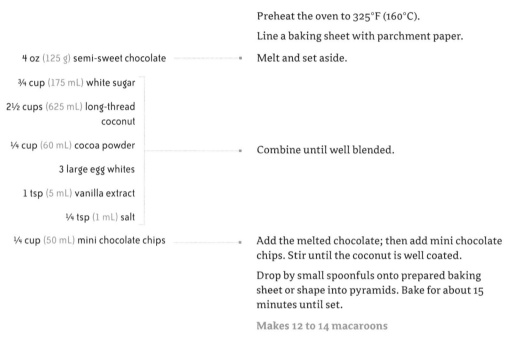

Preheat the oven to 325°F (160°C).

Line a baking sheet with parchment paper.

4 oz (125 g) semi-sweet chocolate — Melt and set aside.

¾ cup (175 mL) white sugar

2½ cups (625 mL) long-thread coconut

¼ cup (60 mL) cocoa powder — Combine until well blended.

3 large egg whites

1 tsp (5 mL) vanilla extract

¼ tsp (1 mL) salt

¼ cup (50 mL) mini chocolate chips — Add the melted chocolate; then add mini chocolate chips. Stir until the coconut is well coated.

Drop by small spoonfuls onto prepared baking sheet or shape into pyramids. Bake for about 15 minutes until set.

Makes 12 to 14 macaroons

tip: These are better underbaked than overbaked.

Gingerbread Men and Women Cookies for Christmas

from *Let Me in the Kitchen*

After a recent Christmas season, I got several requests for this recipe. Here it is! Enjoy!

Preheat oven to 375°F (190°C).

⅔ cup (150 mL) butter, softened — Cream butter.

½ cup (125 mL) brown sugar, well packed — Add sugar a little at a time until fluffy.

2 tsp (10 mL) ground ginger
1 tsp (5 mL) cinnamon
½ tsp (2 mL) ground cloves
1 tsp (5 mL) salt
— Add spices and salt.

1 egg — Add and beat until blended.

¾ cup (175 mL) molasses — Add and mix well.

3 cups (750 mL) flour
1 tsp (5 mL) baking soda
½ tsp (2 mL) baking powder
— Sift together and mix into above.

Cover bowl with plastic wrap and chill for half an hour.

flour — Sprinkle a bread board with flour.

Roll dough to about ⅛ inch (3 mm). Use cookie cutters to cut out shapes.

Bake in preheated oven for 8 to 10 minutes.

Decorate as desired.

Makes 20 to 24 gingerbread people.

Potato Knishes

Late in life, Grandma Faye suggested that we make these with frozen puff pastry dough, and it certainly was a lot easier. Grandma was more flexible as she got older!

Dough

2 cups (500 mL) flour

1 tsp (5 mL) baking powder

½ cup (125 mL) cold water

pinch of salt

¼ cup (50 mL) corn oil

Mix all ingredients in a bowl.

Remove to a floured board.

Knead for 5 minutes. Dough must be soft.

Divide into 2 rounds. Cover and keep warm for 15 minutes.

Filling

5 lb (2.2 kg) potatoes

Boil potatoes.

4 large onions

oil

pinch of baking soda

Fry onions in a little oil. Add baking soda to soften. Cook onions until browned.

1 tsp (5 mL) salt

Mash potatoes well and add onions and salt.

Preheat the oven to 350°F (175°C).

Roll dough into logs, then cut with the back of your hand into 2-inch (5-cm) pieces. Roll 1 ball of dough at a time as thin as you can. Place half of potato mixture on edge of dough and roll up. Cut into 1-inch (2.5-cm) slices with side of hand (do not use knife).

Bake in preheated oven for 20 minutes.

Makes 40 knishes

Carrot Apple Passover Kugel

I first tasted this recipe at Paula Brooks' Seder. She generously shared the recipe with me, although she forgets doing so.

Preheat the oven to 350°F (175°C).

Butter a 13- × 9-inch (3.5-L) casserole dish.

5 egg yolks

¾ cup (175 mL) butter, melted

1 cup (250 mL) slivered almonds, toasted

2 large apples, peeled and grated

1½ cups (360 mL) grated carrots

¾ cup (175 mL) matzo meal

3 Tbsp (45 mL) lemon juice

2 tsp (10 mL) cinnamon

Mix all ingredients together.

5 egg whites

¾ cup (185 mL) granulated sugar

Beat egg whites until soft peaks form. Gradually add sugar and beat until absorbed.

Gently fold egg whites into above mixture in 3 additions, to keep the air that has been created.

Gently pour into prepared casserole dish.

½ cup (125 mL) slivered almonds [untoasted]

Sprinkle over top.

Bake in preheated oven about 40 minutes until brown.

Makes 12 servings

Quinoa Pine Nut Pilaf

Quinoa is an Incan seed that looks like a grain. It is high in protein, vitamins and minerals. Because it is not actually a grain, it has recently been decreed kosher for Passover.

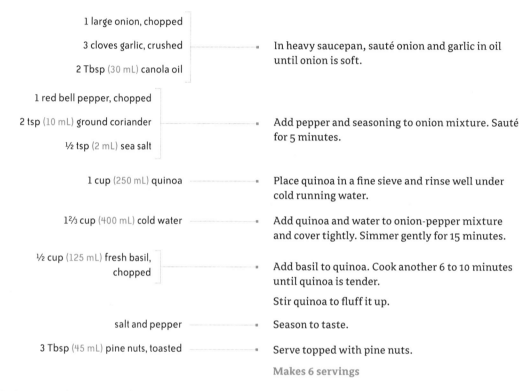

1 large onion, chopped 3 cloves garlic, crushed 2 Tbsp (30 mL) canola oil	In heavy saucepan, sauté onion and garlic in oil until onion is soft.
1 red bell pepper, chopped 2 tsp (10 mL) ground coriander ½ tsp (2 mL) sea salt	Add pepper and seasoning to onion mixture. Sauté for 5 minutes.
1 cup (250 mL) quinoa	Place quinoa in a fine sieve and rinse well under cold running water.
1⅔ cup (400 mL) cold water	Add quinoa and water to onion-pepper mixture and cover tightly. Simmer gently for 15 minutes.
½ cup (125 mL) fresh basil, chopped	Add basil to quinoa. Cook another 6 to 10 minutes until quinoa is tender. Stir quinoa to fluff it up.
salt and pepper	Season to taste.
3 Tbsp (45 mL) pine nuts, toasted	Serve topped with pine nuts.

Makes 6 servings

tip: To toast pine nuts, preheat oven to 350°F (180°C). Spread nuts on an unoiled baking sheet and bake until golden brown, 4 to 5 minutes. Watch them carefully, as they can burn quickly!

Passover Truffle Brownies

This recipe was given to me by Eve Sheftel, one of my favorite customers. It has become everyone's favorite Passover dessert. Everyone tells me that they would like to make it year-round! It's chewy and chocolatey at the same time.

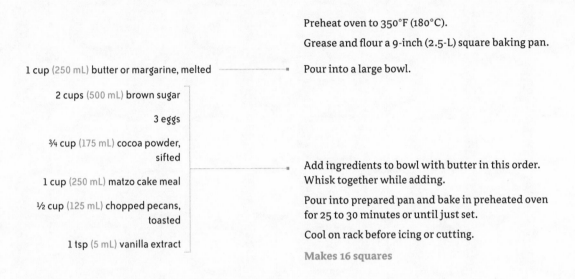

Preheat oven to 350°F (180°C).

Grease and flour a 9-inch (2.5-L) square baking pan.

1 cup (250 mL) butter or margarine, melted — Pour into a large bowl.

2 cups (500 mL) brown sugar

3 eggs

¾ cup (175 mL) cocoa powder, sifted

1 cup (250 mL) matzo cake meal

½ cup (125 mL) chopped pecans, toasted

1 tsp (5 mL) vanilla extract

Add ingredients to bowl with butter in this order. Whisk together while adding.

Pour into prepared pan and bake in preheated oven for 25 to 30 minutes or until just set.

Cool on rack before icing or cutting.

Makes 16 squares

tip: You can glaze the brownies with Lazy Gourmet Glaze (see page 210) or top them with Incredible Chocolate Icing (see page 199).

CHAPTER SIX: PART ONE

Entrées

Fish and Seafood

Bouillabaisse

from *Mama Never Cooked Like This*

This bouillabaisse is one of my most popular dinners. We have it all the time. After 25 years, it's still a keeper and I haven't made any changes to the recipe. Serve with Caesar Salad (see page 53) and Honey Molasses Sweet Bread (see page 178).

Soup

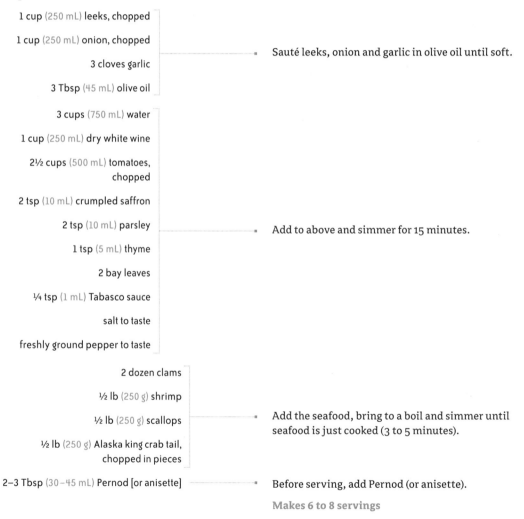

1 cup (250 mL) leeks, chopped

1 cup (250 mL) onion, chopped

3 cloves garlic

3 Tbsp (45 mL) olive oil

Sauté leeks, onion and garlic in olive oil until soft.

3 cups (750 mL) water

1 cup (250 mL) dry white wine

2½ cups (500 mL) tomatoes, chopped

2 tsp (10 mL) crumpled saffron

2 tsp (10 mL) parsley

1 tsp (5 mL) thyme

2 bay leaves

¼ tsp (1 mL) Tabasco sauce

salt to taste

freshly ground pepper to taste

Add to above and simmer for 15 minutes.

2 dozen clams

½ lb (250 g) shrimp

½ lb (250 g) scallops

½ lb (250 g) Alaska king crab tail, chopped in pieces

Add the seafood, bring to a boil and simmer until seafood is just cooked (3 to 5 minutes).

2–3 Tbsp (30–45 mL) Pernod [or anisette]

Before serving, add Pernod (or anisette).

Makes 6 to 8 servings

Salmon Teriyaki

from *Mama Never Cooked Like This*

Since this recipe was developed for *Mama* ..., I have added the thickened glaze. I'm sure you'll enjoy it as much as my family does.

1 cup (250 mL) soy sauce or tamari sauce

¼ cup (50 mL) mirin or sherry

2 Tbsp (30 mL) sugar — Combine ingredients.

2 cloves garlic, crushed

2 Tbsp (30 mL) grated fresh ginger

2 lb (1 kg) salmon fillets — Marinate salmon fillets in teriyaki mixture for 10 minutes.

Place fillets on broiler pan and broil for 10 to 12 minutes. Baste as necessary.

Finish with either the new glaze or Honey Mustard Sauce (recipe follows).

New Glaze — Heat excess teriyaki mixture in small saucepan.

1 Tbsp (15 mL) cornstarch

3 Tbsp (45 mL) cold water — Dissolve cornstarch in cold water. Add to hot teriyaki mixture.

Whisk until thickened.

Pour over cooked fish once it is on the serving platter. Serve with rice.

Makes 6 servings

Honey Mustard Sauce

from *The Expo 86 Cookbook*

one 6-oz (170-g) jar Dijon mustard

1½ cups (360 mL) mayonnaise

2 Tbsp (30 mL) honey — Whisk together.

2 Tbsp (30 mL) freshly squeezed lemon juice

Serve with Salmon Teriyaki if you have not put on the new glaze.

Makes 2 cups (500 mL)

Spectacular Decorated Baked Salmon

from *The Expo 86 Cookbook*

Version One

Preheat the oven to 375°F (190°C).

one 6-lb (2.7-kg) spring or sockeye salmon, stuffed

Fish should be butterflied (head and tail on, but centre bone removed).

Make wrapper for fish by folding edges of 2 large pieces of foil together.

Place salmon, stuffed with your favorite stuffing, on foil so that back is up and stuffed portion is down.

½ cup (125 mL) white wine

juice of 1 lemon

light sprinkling of salt and pepper

Combine and brush over back of fish.

Wrap foil loosely around fish, leaving room inside for steam to circulate. Bake 1 hour and 20 minutes.

To check for doneness, open foil at top and insert small knife in flesh. If it flakes, it is ready. If not, cover and return to oven for 5 to 10 minutes. Try not to overcook!

Makes 12 servings

Version Two

one 6-lb (2.7-kg) salmon, prepared as above

Remove skin while fish is still warm (it will peel off). Cool to room temperature.

Wrap in plastic wrap, and chill 4 to 5 hours or overnight.

Place salmon on large platter on bed of lettuce or spinach leaves.

1 large long English cucumber

2 large lemons

Slice cucumber and lemons as thinly as possible. Cover the fish as completely as possible with the cucumber slices to give the appearance of scales. Place lemon slices at random or down the centre of the fish.

Serve with Lime Mayonnaise or Cucumber-Dill Sauce (recipes follow).

Makes 12 servings

Lime Mayonnaise

from *The Expo 86 Cookbook*

2 large egg yolks

2 tsp (10 mL) Dijon mustard

1 tsp (5 mL) lime juice

freshly ground white pepper to taste

> Combine in a food processor or blender, or beat well with a whisk.

½ cup (125 mL) peanut or olive oil

> Add to above, 1 drop at a time, until thickened.

1–2 Tbsp (15–30 mL) lime juice

¼ tsp (1 mL) salt

freshly ground white pepper to taste

rind of 1 lime, finely grated

> Combine and add to above.

Serve in a small bowl. Decorate with a lime slice.

Makes ¾ cup (175 mL)

Cucumber-Dill Sauce

from *The Expo 86 Cookbook*

¼ long English cucumber

> Chop very fine.

¼ tsp (1 mL) salt

> Toss cucumber with salt. Let stand for 15 minutes.

½ cup (125 mL) plain yogurt

1 cup (250 mL) sour cream

1 tsp (5 mL) lemon juice

3 green onions, finely chopped [white part only]

2 tsp (10 mL) chopped fresh dill or 1 tsp (5 mL) dried dill

> Combine thoroughly.

white pepper

> Add to taste to yogurt mixture.

substitution: A lower-calorie accompaniment to any fresh fish dish—reverse the proportions and use 1 cup (250 mL) of plain yogurt to ½ cup (125 mL) of sour cream.

Squeeze water from cucumber and add to above.

Makes 2 cups (500 mL)

Fresh Halibut with Basil and Parsley Sauce

from *The Expo 86 Cookbook*

This is a stunning way to serve halibut for a special treat. I first made this dish for my friend Don Harron and it remains a memorable meal for me!

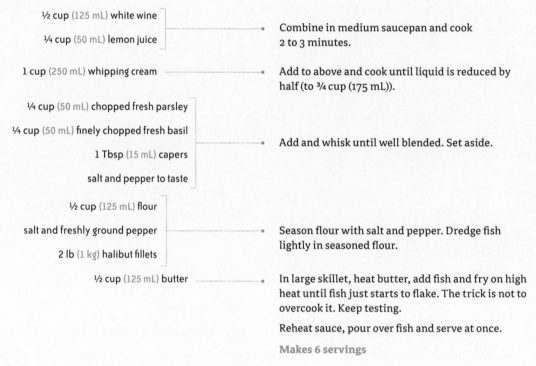

½ cup (125 mL) white wine

¼ cup (50 mL) lemon juice

Combine in medium saucepan and cook 2 to 3 minutes.

1 cup (250 mL) whipping cream

Add to above and cook until liquid is reduced by half (to ¾ cup (175 mL)).

¼ cup (50 mL) chopped fresh parsley

¼ cup (50 mL) finely chopped fresh basil

1 Tbsp (15 mL) capers

salt and pepper to taste

Add and whisk until well blended. Set aside.

½ cup (125 mL) flour

salt and freshly ground pepper

2 lb (1 kg) halibut fillets

Season flour with salt and pepper. Dredge fish lightly in seasoned flour.

½ cup (125 mL) butter

In large skillet, heat butter, add fish and fry on high heat until fish just starts to flake. The trick is not to overcook it. Keep testing.

Reheat sauce, pour over fish and serve at once.

Makes 6 servings

tip: For this recipe, fillets are preferable to steaks. If fresh halibut is in season, treat yourself to a thick centre cut. To cut back on the fat, serve the sauce on the side.

Susie and Peter's Hazelnut Lemon Halibut

from The Expo 86 Cookbook

This is one of my favorite recipes! It is also excellent with snapper, cod or any white fish. I have made this dish and served it as a cold entrée at luncheons. It's always a hit.

Preheat the oven to 350°F (180°C).

1 cup (250 mL) fine dry breadcrumbs

½ cup (125 mL) coarsely chopped hazelnuts

salt and pepper to taste — Mix together and set aside.

grated rind of 1 lemon

2–3 Tbsp (30–45 mL) chopped fresh parsley

juice of 1 lemon

2 lb (1 kg) halibut fillets — Squeeze lemon over halibut.

½ cup (125 mL) flour

salt and pepper — Season flour to taste with salt and pepper. Dredge fish in seasoned flour.

1 egg

2 Tbsp (30 mL) half-and-half — Beat together. Dip fish in egg mixture.

Now dip in hazelnut mixture.

4–6 Tbsp (60–90 mL) butter or oil, or a combination — Fry halibut in butter or oil, 3 to 4 minutes on each side, depending on thickness of fish, until light brown and crisp.

Transfer fish to baking sheet. Bake in preheated oven 8 to 10 minutes.

lemon slices

fresh parsley — Garnish with lemon slices and parsley springs and serve immediately.

Makes 6 servings

Halibut with Sweet Red Pepper Sauce

from *The Expo 86 Cookbook*

This sauce is great over any fish.

3–4 red bell peppers, roasted and peeled [see Roasted Red Pepper and Tomato Soup, page 46]

• Purée in food processor or blender.

2 Tbsp (30 mL) whipping cream
¼ tsp (1 mL) sugar
2 tsp (10 mL) fresh lemon juice
2 Tbsp (30 mL) unsalted butter, softened

• Add to peppers and process until smooth. Place in top of double boiler and keep warm.

2 lb (1 kg) halibut fillets or steaks

• Poach or fry fish. When it flakes easily, pour sauce over fish.

Makes 6 servings

Sea Bass with Lime Ginger Sauce

My friend Michiko Sahata first made this dish for my family in Mexico. Now we make it all the time!

Preheat the oven to 400°F (200°C).

one 8-oz (125-mL) jar preserved whole ginger in syrup
2 limes, juiced

• Process in a mini processor or blender.

twelve 4-oz (125-g) pieces sea bass

• Bake in preheated oven for 4 minutes.

Spread the sauce evenly and not too thickly over the fish.

Place under broiler for 7 to 10 minutes until fish just flakes and sauce caramelizes.

Makes 12 servings

substitution: Sea bass is now considered an endangered species, so I make this dish with halibut, sablefish or snapper. Any white fish will work!

Clams or Mussels in Black Bean Sauce

from *The Expo 86 Cookbook*

A wonderful combination of West Coast ingredients and Chinese cooking technique.

1½ lb (750 g) fresh clams	Scrub well.
1 Tbsp (15 mL) black beans	
1 clove garlic, crushed	
1 tsp (5 L) grated fresh ginger	Blend well in blender or food processor.
2 tsp (10 mL) oil	
1 Tbsp (15 mL) oil	In large skillet, heat oil until it smokes.
1 tsp (5 mL) diced onion	Brown onions in oil, then add black bean mixture.
4 strips red bell pepper	
4 strips green bell pepper	Add peppers to skillet.
	Add clams to skillet. Cover, uncover and stir, then cover again. (This hastens cooking time.)
1 tsp (5 mL) honey	
1 Tbsp (15 mL) soy sauce	
1 Tbsp (15 mL) dry white wine	Combine in small bowl and add as soon as clams open.
½ tsp (2 mL) cornstarch, dissolved in 2 tsp (10 mL) cold water	
pinch of white pepper	Add pepper and stir until clams are coated with sauce.
1 tsp (5 mL) oil	Add to give clams a shine.
2 sprigs cilantro	Garnish with cilantro and serve.

Serves 2 as a main course or 4 as an appetizer

Halibut Parcels with Tomato Cilantro Sauce

from *The Lazy Gourmet*

Impress your friends with this gorgeous main course, another favorite recipe from the bistro. It's much easier to make than the finished product suggests. We also make this dish with tofu instead of the fish—pleasing our vegetarian friends immensely.

Preheat the oven to 350°C (175°F).

⅔ cup (150 mL) halved and seeded tomatoes (about 3 Roma tomatoes)

Place tomatoes on a baking sheet and bake until they are dried, 30 to 40 minutes. Cool and coarsely chop.

6 Tbsp (90 mL) chopped cilantro

2 Tbsp (30 mL) garlic

1 Tbsp (15 mL) ginger

4 Tbsp (60 mL) green onions

In a food processor or blender, mix the cilantro, garlic, ginger and green onion.

1 Tbsp (15 mL) sesame oil

Blend in sesame oil until a paste is formed. (Set aside 2 Tbsp (30 mL) of this paste for the sauce.)

eight 4-oz (113-g) halibut fillets

Spread the paste evenly over one side of each piece of fish.

8 sheets rice paper [10-inch (25-cm) rounds]

Working with one sheet of rice paper at a time, soak it for 15 to 20 seconds in warm water. Remove and place it on a clean surface. Place a piece of halibut on the center of the rice sheet. Fold the bottom, sides and top over to completely wrap the halibut.

2 Tbsp (30 mL) vegetable oil

In a very hot sauté pan with the oil, sear the parcels. Finish them in the oven for approximately 10 minutes, or until they are lightly browned.

In a sauté pan, sauté the 2 Tbsp (30 mL) of reserved paste with the roasted tomatoes.

1 cup (250 mL) white wine

½ cup (125 mL) fish stock

6 Tbsp (90 mL) butter, cubed

Add white wine and fish stock and bring to a boil. Reduce heat and swirl in butter.

To serve, place the parcels on a platter, and pour sauce over and around them.

Makes 8 parcels

Baked Sea Bass or Halibut with Pistachio Crust and Orange Basil Sauce

Another recipe guaranteed to wow your friends!

Preheat the oven to 350°F (175°C).

2 cups (500 mL) pistachios, coarsely ground

2 cups (500 mL) *panko* [Japanese breadcrumbs]

Mix pistachios and *panko* on a plate.

6 egg whites, lightly beaten

Place egg whites in a shallow pan.

eight 4-oz (113-g) sea bass or halibut fillets

salt and freshly ground white pepper

Season fillets to taste with salt and white pepper. Dip 1 side of each fillet in egg white, then into the pistachio-breadcrumb mixture to make a crust.

4 Tbsp (60 mL) vegetable oil

Heat oil in a sauté pan, and sear the crusted sides of the fillets. Place on a baking sheet, and finish in the oven for 15 to 18 minutes or until fish is flaky.

3 cups (750 mL) Orange Basil Sauce [recipe follows]

Serve the sea bass on a platter and drizzle the Orange Basil Sauce over and around the fish.

tip: *Panko* are Japanese breadcrumbs; they are lighter and fluffier than regular bread crumbs.

Makes 8 servings

Orange Basil Sauce

from The Lazy Gourmet

2 cups (500 mL) orange juice

1 cup (250mL) white wine

2 Tbsp (30 mL) honey

1 cup (250 mL) whipping cream

2 tsp (10 mL) chopped orange rind

½ cup (125 mL) orange segments

salt and black pepper

In a saucepan, combine orange juice, white wine, honey and whipping cream. Bring to a boil, then reduce heat and add orange rind and segments. Season to taste with salt and pepper. Continue to cook until sauce is reduced by about one-third.

¼ cup (50 mL) butter, cubed

2 Tbsp (30 mL) chopped fresh basil

Remove from heat, swirl in butter and add basil.

Makes 3 cups (750 mL)

Halibut with Tomato, Basil and Garlic Sauce

A delicious low-fat main course! This is a new recipe great for those on restricted diets. I like to use organic canned tomatoes. They're tastier and have less salt.

Preheat oven to 425°F (220°C).

Spray a 13- × 9-inch (3.5-L) glass casserole dish with cooking oil. Cut a piece of parchment the size of the dish and spray with cooking oil and set aside.

two 28-oz (796-mL) cans whole tomatoes

Process tomatoes in blender. Place in large saucepan and boil uncovered until sauce is thickened.

salt and pepper

Add salt and pepper to taste.

1½ lb (750 g) halibut, cut into 6 portions

2 Tbsp (30 mL) white wine or lemon juice

Arrange 6 fish pieces in casserole dish and sprinkle with white wine or lemon juice.

½ cup (125 mL) vegetable broth

Bring vegetable broth to a boil and pour over the fish.

Put oiled paper directly on the fish and bake in preheated oven for 10 to 12 minutes.

3 large cloves garlic, minced

Remove the fish gently and set aside.

1 large bunch fresh basil, coarsely chopped

Pour cooking liquid back into the tomato sauce. Add minced garlic and basil. Boil the sauce until it is thick again.

Coat the fish with the sauce and serve hot.

Makes 6 servings

Halibut with Lemon Ginger Chili Marinade

Marinade

1 Tbsp (15 mL) finely minced lemon peel

⅓ cup (75 mL) freshly squeezed lemon juice

½ cup (125 mL) dry white wine

2 Tbsp (30 mL) canola oil

2 Tbsp (30 mL) soy sauce [I like Yamasa]

1 Tbsp (15 mL) oyster sauce

½ tsp (2 mL) Asian chili sauce

1 Tbsp (15 mL) finely minced fresh ginger [I grate mine]

2 cloves crushed garlic

Mix all together.

2 lb (1 kg) halibut [or any white fish] fillets, cut into 6 pieces

Marinate fish 15 to 20 minutes; turn to coat. Keep refrigerated until ready to cook.

Broil 6 inches (15 cm) from element, 10 to 12 minutes, until fish just flakes. Continue to coat with marinade as fish cooks.

Makes 6 to 8 servings

tip: Be careful not to overcook the halibut. I find that one minute too long can make a difference between a moist fish and a dry one. It's best to use fresh halibut for perfect results.

My Thai Green Curry Halibut

This is a recipe that I learned how to make at a cooking class in Phuket, Thailand. Serve with fragrant jasmine rice. Enjoy!

1 cup (250 mL) coconut milk

1½ oz (30 g) Thai green curry paste

Cook down until milk starts to separate.

3 cups (750 mL) coconut milk

6 small Thai eggplants, cubed

2½ Tbsp (37 mL) fish sauce

2 tsp (10 mL) palm sugar

2 pieces kaffir lime leaf

Add and cook until thickened.

one 3-lb (1.5-kg) halibut, cut into chunks

1 Tbsp (15 mL) sweet basil leaves

Add and cook 3 to 5 minutes.

Makes 6 to 8 servings

substitution: You can sometimes find the small Thai eggplants in Asian markets. They're delicious. Otherwise, stick to the small Japanese eggplants (use 2 of them). They're sweeter than the larger variety.

Sablefish *with* Miso Glaze

This is our family's favorite fish. I serve it for fancy dinner parties and it always gets rave reviews. I never tell anyone how easy it is to make! Serve with jasmine rice and steamed vegetables.

Marinade

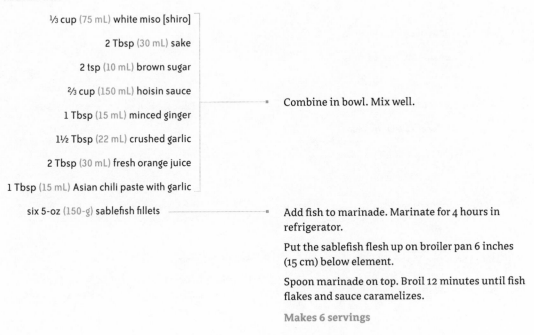

⅓ cup (75 mL) white miso [shiro]

2 Tbsp (30 mL) sake

2 tsp (10 mL) brown sugar

⅔ cup (150 mL) hoisin sauce

1 Tbsp (15 mL) minced ginger

1½ Tbsp (22 mL) crushed garlic

2 Tbsp (30 mL) fresh orange juice

1 Tbsp (15 mL) Asian chili paste with garlic

Combine in bowl. Mix well.

six 5-oz (150-g) sablefish fillets

Add fish to marinade. Marinate for 4 hours in refrigerator.

Put the sablefish flesh up on broiler pan 6 inches (15 cm) below element.

Spoon marinade on top. Broil 12 minutes until fish flakes and sauce caramelizes.

Makes 6 servings

Easy Pad Thai with Shrimp or Salmon

This is another recipe developed over the course of a summer at the lake. My daughter Mira loves it when I make it with leftover salmon instead of the shrimp. Given that shrimp is so plentiful in Thailand and salmon is so plentiful in British Columbia, the substitution makes sense.

Sauce

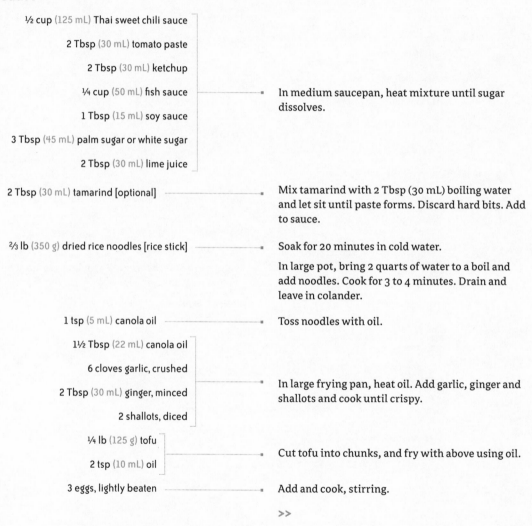

½ cup (125 mL) Thai sweet chili sauce

2 Tbsp (30 mL) tomato paste

2 Tbsp (30 mL) ketchup

¼ cup (50 mL) fish sauce

1 Tbsp (15 mL) soy sauce

3 Tbsp (45 mL) palm sugar or white sugar

2 Tbsp (30 mL) lime juice

> In medium saucepan, heat mixture until sugar dissolves.

2 Tbsp (30 mL) tamarind [optional]

> Mix tamarind with 2 Tbsp (30 mL) boiling water and let sit until paste forms. Discard hard bits. Add to sauce.

⅔ lb (350 g) dried rice noodles [rice stick]

> Soak for 20 minutes in cold water.
>
> In large pot, bring 2 quarts of water to a boil and add noodles. Cook for 3 to 4 minutes. Drain and leave in colander.

1 tsp (5 mL) canola oil

> Toss noodles with oil.

1½ Tbsp (22 mL) canola oil

6 cloves garlic, crushed

2 Tbsp (30 mL) ginger, minced

2 shallots, diced

> In large frying pan, heat oil. Add garlic, ginger and shallots and cook until crispy.

¼ lb (125 g) tofu

2 tsp (10 mL) oil

> Cut tofu into chunks, and fry with above using oil.

3 eggs, lightly beaten

> Add and cook, stirring.

>>

1 lb (500 g) uncooked shrimp — Add and cook 2 to 3 minutes. Add noodles and sauce, and toss and cook until noodles have absorbed sauce.

3 limes, cut into wedges

cilantro leaves

½ cup (125 mL) unsalted, roasted chopped peanuts — Place on platter and garnish with these items.

4 green onions, diced

7 oz (200 g) fresh bean sprouts

Makes about 6 servings

Seared Sesame Tuna with Ponzu Sauce

This is another summer favorite at the lake. It's so easy and can be done on the barbecue as well. I serve it with Spinach Mushroom Gratin (see page 85) or Mixed Wild Rices and Wild Mushrooms (see page 80).

Marinade

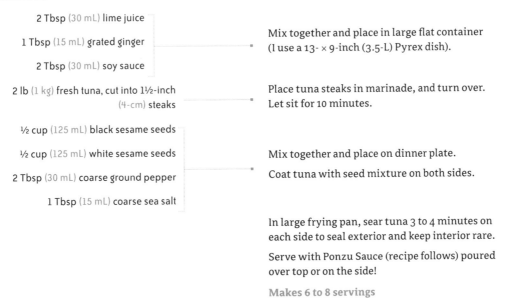

2 Tbsp (30 mL) lime juice

1 Tbsp (15 mL) grated ginger — Mix together and place in large flat container (I use a 13- × 9-inch (3.5-L) Pyrex dish).

2 Tbsp (30 mL) soy sauce

2 lb (1 kg) fresh tuna, cut into 1½-inch (4-cm) steaks — Place tuna steaks in marinade, and turn over. Let sit for 10 minutes.

½ cup (125 mL) black sesame seeds

½ cup (125 mL) white sesame seeds — Mix together and place on dinner plate.

2 Tbsp (30 mL) coarse ground pepper — Coat tuna with seed mixture on both sides.

1 Tbsp (15 mL) coarse sea salt

In large frying pan, sear tuna 3 to 4 minutes on each side to seal exterior and keep interior rare.

Serve with Ponzu Sauce (recipe follows) poured over top or on the side!

Makes 6 to 8 servings

Ponzu Sauce

½ cup (125 mL) lemon juice

⅓ cup (75 mL) sugar

4 Tbsp (60 mL) mirin

2 Tbsp (30 mL) soy sauce · · · · · · · · · Mix together until sugar is dissolved.

2 tsp (10 mL) sambal oelek

2 tsp (10 mL) minced ginger

1 tsp (5 mL) lemon rind

Makes 1 cup (250 mL)

CHAPTER SIX: PART TWO

Entrées

Beef and Lamb

Beef Stroganoff

from *The Expo 86 Cookbook*

This old-time favorite has always been popular! Best made at the last minute. Serve with a steamed green vegetable.

2 lb (1 kg) sirloin, sliced ¼ inch (5 mm) thick ½ cup (125 mL) butter	Brown strips of meat well in butter. Remove from pan, but keep warm.
2 cups (500 mL) coarsely chopped onion 2 cloves garlic, minced	Add to pan and cook until tender.
½ lb (250 g) mushrooms, sliced	Add and cook until tender.
2 Tbsp (30 mL) flour salt and pepper 1½ cups (360 mL) beef stock	Stir flour into vegetables. Season to taste with salt and pepper. Add to beef stock and cook, stirring constantly, until thickened.
¼ cup (50 mL) dry white wine 1 cup (250 mL) sour cream 1 tsp (5 mL) Worcestershire sauce handful of chopped fresh parsley	Combine and add.
1 lb (500 g) dry fettuccine or 1½ lb (750 g) fresh 2–3 Tbsp (30–45 mL) butter	Cook fettuccine in boiling, salted water—8 to 10 minutes for dry, 5 to 6 minutes for fresh. Drain and toss with butter. Return meat to pan and cook until reheated.
chopped fresh parsley	Serve meat on a bed of noodles. Sprinkle with parsley before serving.

Makes 6 to 8 servings

Lynn's Couscous

from *Food to Grow On*

Thanks to my sister Lynn for another terrific recipe!

¼ cup (50 mL) butter

2 medium onions, chopped

Sauté onions in butter until translucent.

1 cup (250 mL) chopped celery

2 tsp (10 mL) ground coriander

2 tsp (10 mL) cinnamon

¼ tsp (1 mL) cayenne

¼ tsp (1 mL) saffron

Add to onion and cook additional 5 minutes.

2 lb (1 kg) beef, cut into small cubes

two 19-oz (540-mL) cans plum tomatoes

one 14-oz (398-mL) can chickpeas

6 carrots, cut into chunks

4 turnips, cut into chunks

4 small zucchini, cut into chunks

2 acorn squashes, cut into small pieces

2 red peppers, cut into chunks

2 sticks cinnamon, cut into pieces

3 Tbsp (45 mL) chopped fresh parley

Add to onion and celery mixture and bring to a boil. Simmer for 30 minutes.

2 lb (1 kg) couscous

8 cups (2 L) boiling salted water

Put couscous in water. Let sit for 5 minutes.

4 Tbsp (60 mL) olive oil

Put in a large skillet and toss with couscous for 5 minutes on medium heat.

Serve vegetable and beef mixture on a bed of couscous.

Makes 8 to 10 servings

Beef Bourgignon

from *The Expo 86 Cookbook*

The burgundy wine elevates the chuck beef to a gourmet extravagance. A meal in itself! Serve with a light salad.

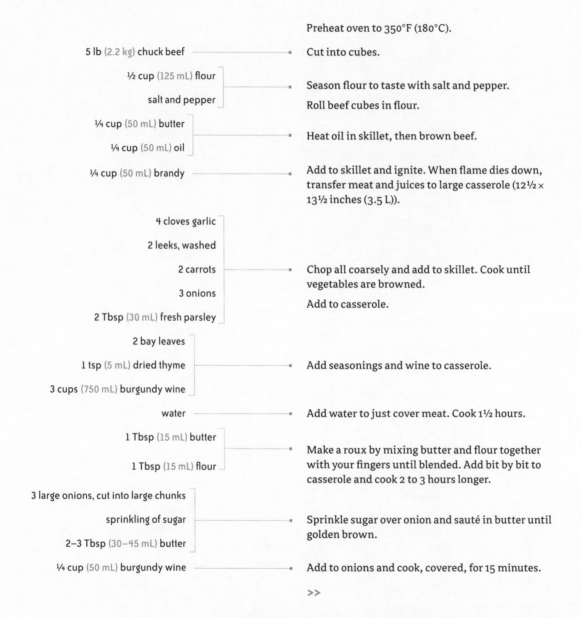

Preheat oven to 350°F (180°C).

5 lb (2.2 kg) chuck beef — Cut into cubes.

½ cup (125 mL) flour
salt and pepper — Season flour to taste with salt and pepper.
Roll beef cubes in flour.

¼ cup (50 mL) butter
¼ cup (50 mL) oil — Heat oil in skillet, then brown beef.

¼ cup (50 mL) brandy — Add to skillet and ignite. When flame dies down, transfer meat and juices to large casserole (12½ × 13½ inches (3.5 L)).

4 cloves garlic
2 leeks, washed
2 carrots — Chop all coarsely and add to skillet. Cook until vegetables are browned.
3 onions
2 Tbsp (30 mL) fresh parsley — Add to casserole.

2 bay leaves
1 tsp (5 mL) dried thyme — Add seasonings and wine to casserole.
3 cups (750 mL) burgundy wine

water — Add water to just cover meat. Cook 1½ hours.

1 Tbsp (15 mL) butter
1 Tbsp (15 mL) flour — Make a roux by mixing butter and flour together with your fingers until blended. Add bit by bit to casserole and cook 2 to 3 hours longer.

3 large onions, cut into large chunks
sprinkling of sugar — Sprinkle sugar over onion and sauté in butter until golden brown.
2–3 Tbsp (30–45 mL) butter

¼ cup (50 mL) burgundy wine — Add to onions and cook, covered, for 15 minutes.

>>

1 lb (500 g) mushroom caps	Brown mushrooms in butter until just tender, turning to cook both sides.
2 Tbsp (30 mL) butter	
juice of ½ lemon	Sprinkle over mushrooms.
chopped fresh parsley	To serve, add onions to casserole, decorate top with mushrooms and sprinkle with parsley.

Makes 10 to 12 servings

Beef Tenderloin with Black Bean Sauce

This is a variation of a recipe I first made in a class I took with Hugh Carpenter, my favorite fusion chef.

Sauce

1 cup (250 mL) black bean sauce	
1 cup (250 mL) soy sauce	
1 cup (250 mL) hoisin sauce	Mix together.
½ cup (125 mL) balsamic vinegar	
½ cup (125 mL) sesame oil	
¼ cup (50 mL) sugar	

one 3–4 lb (1.5–2 kg) tenderloin roast	Marinate tenderloin roast for 2 hours in sauce.
	Preheat oven to 500°F (260°C).
	Place in preheated oven for 5 minutes. Reduce heat to 400°F (200°C) and cook for 15 to 20 minutes until roast tests done.

Makes 8 to 10 servings

variation: This can also be made on the barbecue. It works well on individual steaks as well.

Roast Rack of Lamb with a Mushroom Crust

from *The Lazy Gourmet*

Rack of lamb is a great entrée for special occasions. For ease of preparation, order it "frenched" from your butcher. Frenching trims the meat, fat and gristle from the end of the bone to expose it for an attractive presentation.

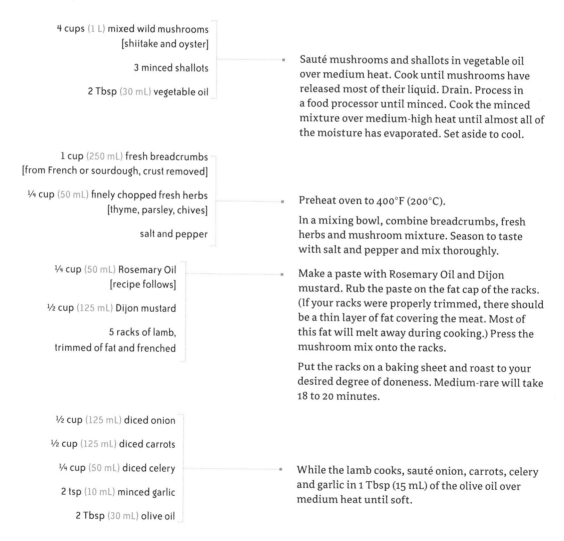

4 cups (1 L) mixed wild mushrooms [shiitake and oyster]

3 minced shallots

2 Tbsp (30 mL) vegetable oil

Sauté mushrooms and shallots in vegetable oil over medium heat. Cook until mushrooms have released most of their liquid. Drain. Process in a food processor until minced. Cook the minced mixture over medium-high heat until almost all of the moisture has evaporated. Set aside to cool.

1 cup (250 mL) fresh breadcrumbs [from French or sourdough, crust removed]

¼ cup (50 mL) finely chopped fresh herbs [thyme, parsley, chives]

salt and pepper

Preheat oven to 400°F (200°C).

In a mixing bowl, combine breadcrumbs, fresh herbs and mushroom mixture. Season to taste with salt and pepper and mix thoroughly.

¼ cup (50 mL) Rosemary Oil [recipe follows]

½ cup (125 mL) Dijon mustard

5 racks of lamb, trimmed of fat and frenched

Make a paste with Rosemary Oil and Dijon mustard. Rub the paste on the fat cap of the racks. (If your racks were properly trimmed, there should be a thin layer of fat covering the meat. Most of this fat will melt away during cooking.) Press the mushroom mix onto the racks.

Put the racks on a baking sheet and roast to your desired degree of doneness. Medium-rare will take 18 to 20 minutes.

½ cup (125 mL) diced onion

½ cup (125 mL) diced carrots

¼ cup (50 mL) diced celery

2 tsp (10 mL) minced garlic

2 Tbsp (30 mL) olive oil

While the lamb cooks, sauté onion, carrots, celery and garlic in 1 Tbsp (15 mL) of the olive oil over medium heat until soft.

>>

4 cups (1 L) cooked white beans	Add beans and 2 cups (500 mL) of water. Heat through.
1 Tbsp (15 mL) sherry vinegar	Stir in sherry vinegar and the remaining 1 Tbsp (15 mL) olive oil.
salt and pepper	Season to taste with salt and pepper.
	To serve, mound the bean mixture in the centre of a large platter. Surround it with the racks.
¼ cup (50 mL) Rosemary Oil [recipe follows]	Drizzle more Rosemary Oil over the racks.
	Makes 8 servings

tip: A rack generally has 7 ribs in it. Four to five ribs will usually satisfy one person.

Rosemary Oil

from *The Lazy Gourmet*

2 cups (500 mL) rosemary leaves	Blanch the rosemary leaves in boiling salted water for 30 to 40 seconds. Drain and plunge in ice water to stop it from cooking any further. Drain in a strainer or colander and press gently to squeeze out excess moisture.
1½ cups (360 mL) olive oil	In a blender, process the rosemary and olive oil. Let sit for 24 hours at room temperature.
	Strain and store in the fridge for up to 1 week.
	Makes 2 cups (500 mL)

Balsamic Soy Rack of Lamb

from Food to Grow On

Great served with couscous or roasted potatoes and steamed vegetables.

2 racks of lamb ⋯⋯⋯⋯⋯ Remove fat from top of racks. Using a paring knife, make a small cut between each bone to slightly pierce the meat.

Balsamic Soy Marinade

½ cup (125 mL) balsamic vinegar

½ cup (125 mL) dry red wine

⅓ cup (75 mL) soy sauce ⋯⋯⋯⋯ Combine and pour over lamb. Work the marinade into the slashes in the meat.

3 Tbsp (45 mL) Dijon mustard

6 cloves of garlic, crushed

Cover and refrigerate 4 to 6 hours.

2 Tbsp (30 mL) mixed peppercorns [red, green, white, black], coarsely crushed ⋯⋯⋯ One hour before roasting, mix peppercorns and mustard and rub lamb with the paste.

4 Tbsp (60 mL) honey mustard

Preheat the oven to 450°F (230°C).

Roast lamb until internal temperature is 285°F (140°C)—about 20 minutes. Let rest for 5 minutes, cut into chops and serve on heated platters.

Makes enough to serve 3 to 4

tip: A rack generally has 7 ribs in it. Four to five ribs will usually satisfy one person.

CHAPTER SIX: PART THREE

Entrées

Pasta, Pizza, Risotto and Quiche

Spinach Quiche

from *Mama Never Cooked Like This*

I still get raves for this easy quiche 25 years later. It's a smoother quiche than the Lazy Gourmet Deep-Dish Spinach and Feta Pie.

one 9-inch (23-cm) pie crust, pre-baked 5 minutes at 375°F (190°C) [see No-Fail Pastry, page 208]

Preheat the oven to 350°F (180°).

1 bunch spinach

Wash and stem, then steam spinach until wilted and rinse with cold water to stop the cooking process.

2 eggs

1¼ cups (300 mL) half-and-half

pinch of nutmeg

½ tsp (2 mL) salt

¼ tsp (1 mL) pepper

Mix together in a blender, then add spinach and continue to blend.

1½ cups (360 mL) shredded Jarlsberg cheese or Swiss Emmenthal cheese

Sprinkle on the bottom of pre-baked pie shell.

1 onion, chopped

3 Tbsp (45 mL) oil

Sauté onion in oil, then add to cheese in the pie shell.

Pour spinach mixture over cheese and onion.

Bake in preheated oven for 25 to 30 minutes, until firm to the touch.

Makes 6 to 8 servings

Real Macaroni and Cheese

from *Let Me in the Kitchen*

This is an original recipe from my Grandma Faye. I love seeing macaroni and cheese offered as an accompaniment in very fancy restaurants. It's a comfort food, but also a delicacy!

Preheat oven to 375°F (190°C).

Grease a 13- × 9-inch (3.5-L) casserole dish.

3 cups (750 mL) shredded cheddar cheese — Divide into two amounts: a 2-cup (500-mL) pile and a 1-cup (250-mL) pile.

3 cups (750 mL) macaroni, cooked al dente [vegetable or whole wheat is best] — Set aside.

½ cup (125 mL) butter
6 Tbsp (90 mL) white flour
2 cups (500 mL) milk
1 tsp (5 mL) salt

In a medium pot, melt butter over low heat. Whisk in flour all at once. Keep stirring for 1 minute.

Gradually add milk to sauce, stirring constantly. Sauce will thicken after 5 to 10 minutes.

Stir 2 cups (500 mL) of the cheese into sauce. Add salt.

Turn off heat, add drained noodles and mix.

Pour noodles and sauce into prepared casserole dish and sprinkle with the remaining 1 cup (250 mL) of cheese.

Bake in preheated oven for 25 minutes.

Makes 8 servings

Homemade Pizza

from *Let Me in the Kitchen*

When I first met my husband, Jack, he told me that he had been making this pizza with his son Soleil for years. (He had purchased the first printing of *Let Me in the Kitchen*.) I fell in love with him instantly.

Crust

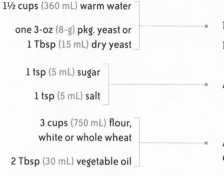

1½ cups (360 mL) warm water

one 3-oz (8-g) pkg. yeast or
1 Tbsp (15 mL) dry yeast

In a large bowl, mix warm water and yeast. Let mixture sit for 5 minutes.

1 tsp (5 mL) sugar

1 tsp (5 mL) salt

Add sugar and salt.

3 cups (750 mL) flour,
white or whole wheat

2 Tbsp (30 mL) vegetable oil

Add flour and oil and mix until blended. Knead the dough with a little flour.

Spread some oil on the inside of another large bowl and put dough in it. Let dough sit for 40 minutes in a warm place. By then it should have doubled in size.

While the dough is rising, make the sauce and prepare the topping.

Sauce

one 5½-oz (156-mL) tin tomato paste

½ cup (125 mL) water

1 clove garlic, crushed

1 tsp (5 mL) granulated sugar

½ tsp (2 mL) salt

½ tsp (2 mL) pepper

1 tsp (5 mL) oregano

1 tsp (5 mL) thyme

1 tsp (5 mL) basil

Put all sauce ingredients into a pot.

Cook sauce on medium heat, stirring occasionally. As soon as it starts to bubble, turn heat to low and simmer for 10 minutes. Remove from heat.

>>

Cheese and Vegetable Topping

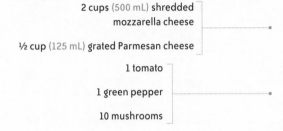

2 cups (500 mL) shredded
mozzarella cheese

½ cup (125 mL) grated Parmesan cheese

Set aside.

1 tomato

1 green pepper

10 mushrooms

Wash tomato, green pepper and mushrooms and cut into thin slices. Set aside.

Preheat the oven to 450°F (230°C).

Oil a baking sheet or pizza pan. When dough is ready, press it onto the pan, turning up the edges to keep the sauce in.

Spread sauce over the crust.

Sprinkle with mozzarella cheese.

Decorate the top with the vegetable slices (or toppings of your choice).

Sprinkle with Parmesan cheese.

Bake for about 15 to 20 minutes until cheese is bubbly and crust is brown.

Makes 4 to 6 servings

tip: Because this recipe is from the kids' cookbook, the cheeses are fairly bland. Feel free to vary them, incorporating your favorites!

variations: Choose other toppings, if you wish: anchovies, olives, et cetera.

Quiche Lorraine

from *The Expo 86 Cookbook*

The first quiche I had in Vancouver was a quiche lorraine. We've now introduced lots of new varieties.

Preheat oven to 450°F (230°C).

one 9- or 10-inch (23- or 25-cm) pie crust,
pre-baked 5 minutes at 375°F (190°C)
[see No-Fail Pastry, page 208]

1 Tbsp (15 mL) butter

1 large onion, sliced in thin rounds

Sauté onion in butter until transparent.

½ cup (125 mL) shredded Gruyère cheese

¾ cup (175 mL) shredded
Emmenthal cheese

¼ cup (50 mL) grated Parmesan cheese

Mix cheeses with onion and sprinkle over crust.

3 eggs

1½ cups (375 mL) whipping cream

¼ tsp (1 mL) nutmeg

½ tsp (2 mL) salt

¼ tsp (1 mL) white pepper

Whisk to blend, and pour over cheese mixture.

Bake 10 minutes; reduce heat to 350°F (180°C) and continue baking for 20 to 30 minutes. Serve hot.

Makes 6 to 8 servings

Quiche Lorraine p. 144

Fresh Salmon Quiche p. 145

Spinach Quiche p. 140

Four-Cheese Quiche with Red Pepper p. 146

Roast Rack of Lamb with a Mushroom Crust   p. 136

Beef Bourgignon   p. 134

Bouillabaisse   p. 114

Fresh Salmon Quiche

from *The Expo 86 Cookbook*

A great way to enjoy our fresh BC salmon. Spring or sockeye are my favorites for this quiche.

Preheat oven to 350°F (180°C).

one 9- or 10-inch (23- or 25-cm) pie crust, pre-baked 5 minutes at 375°F (190°C) [see No-Fail Pastry, page 208]

½ lb (250 g) fresh salmon fillets

¼ cup (50 mL) light cream

3 slices onion

3 peppercorns

¼ cup (50 mL) water

Place salmon in skillet or saucepan. Add remaining ingredients and simmer 8 to 10 minutes until salmon is just firm.

Remove salmon with slotted spoon and set aside. (Liquid can be saved for a soup base.)

2 eggs

1 cup (250 mL) half-and-half

¼ cup (50 mL) whipping cream

salt and white pepper to taste

3 Tbsp (45 mL) cream cheese [optional]

Blend well together.

1½ cups (375 mL) shredded Jarlsberg cheese

Sprinkle cheese on pie crust. Separate salmon gently with hands and layer on cheese.

2 Tbsp (30 mL) capers

Sprinkle capers over salmon and pour cream mixture over all.

Bake 30 to 35 minutes until firm.

Makes 6 to 8 servings

Four-Cheese Quiche with Red Pepper

from *The Expo 86 Cookbook*

Preheat oven to 400°F (200°C).

one 9- or 10-inch (23- or 25-cm) pie crust,
pre-baked 5 minutes at 375°F (190°C)
[see No-Fail Pastry, page 208]

4 oz (125 g) crumbled Roquefort or
blue cheese

3 oz (75 g) shredded Swiss cheese

4 oz (125 g) brie, broken into small bits

Mix together and set aside.

1½ cups (360 mL) whipping cream

3 eggs

pinch of nutmeg

salt and pepper to taste

¼ cup (50 mL) spreadable cream cheese

In blender or food processor, blend well together to make custard.

1 large or 2 small red bell peppers

2 Tbsp (30 mL) butter, melted

Slice peppers into rounds, remove seeds and membrane and sauté in butter until soft.

Sprinkle cheese on crust. Top with sautéed pepper rings. Pour custard over peppers.

Bake 10 minutes. Reduce heat to 350°F (180°C) and continue cooking 20 to 25 minutes until knife inserted in centre comes out clean.

Makes 6 to 8 servings

substitution: This is a very rich quiche. You can use half-and-half or even milk in place of the whipping cream. It will still work.

Lazy Gourmet Deep-Dish Spinach and Feta Pie

from *The Expo 86 Cookbook*

At The Lazy Gourmet, the Greek influence has hit the quiche. Great served hot or at room temperature.

one 9- or 10-inch (23- or 25-cm) pie crust, pre-baked 5 minutes at 375°F (190°C) [see No-Fail Pastry, page 208]	Preheat oven to 350°F (180°C).
1 bunch spinach	Wash, stem and steam spinach until wilted. Squeeze out excess water and chop.
3 Tbsp (45 mL) oil 1 onion, chopped	Heat oil and sauté onion until golden. Toss with spinach.
1 cup (250 mL) shredded Swiss cheese	Mix with onion and spinach.
2 eggs 1¼ cups (300 mL) half-and-half ½ tsp (2 mL) salt ¼ tsp (1 mL) pepper pinch of nutmeg ¼ cup (50 mL) spreadable cream cheese	Mix well with whisk or in a blender to make custard.
6 oz (175 g) grated or crumbled feta cheese 2 medium tomatoes, sliced	Spread onion-spinach-cheese mixture in crust. Top with feta cheese and decorate with tomatoes. Pour on custard, making sure it soaks through to crust. (Use fingers or spoon to spread.) Bake 40 to 45 minutes.

Makes 6 to 8 servings

Cold Spaghettini with Shrimp, Dill, Snow Peas and Red Peppers

from The Expo 86 Cookbook

Great with whole wheat or spelt pasta as well. Serve as a salad course or an entrée on a hot summer's day.

6 cups (1.5 L) cooked spaghettini or linguine

1 lb (500 g) fresh shrimp, shelled, deveined and cooked

2 cups (500 mL) snow peas — Blanch snow peas in boiling water 1 minute, then refresh with cold water until chilled.

1 cup (250 mL) thinly sliced red pepper

½ cup (125 mL) chopped green onion

¼ cup (50 mL) chopped fresh parsley

2 Tbsp (30 mL) chopped fresh dill — Combine in large bowl with cooked shrimp, peas and pasta.

Dressing

2 cloves garlic, crushed

6 Tbsp (90 mL) fresh lemon juice

salt and freshly ground pepper

1 cup (250 mL) light salad oil — Combine, adding salt and pepper to taste and the oil last.

Add to salad and toss. Serve at once.

Makes 6 to 8 servings

Pasta with Sun-Dried Tomatoes

from *Food to Grow On*

Simple to make! The whole wheat and spelt pastas are much tastier than you might expect. Try it ... you'll like it. Just don't overcook the pasta.

4 cups (1 L) pasta [wheat, whole wheat or spelt], cooked	Set aside.
½ cup (125 mL) sun-dried tomatoes 2 cups (500 mL) boiling water	Soak in water, then cut into small pieces. Save water.
1 large onion 1 Tbsp (15 mL) oil 2 cloves garlic	Chop and fry in small batches until dark brown. Add tomatoes and sauté.
1 chili pepper, cut into small pieces [optional]	Add.
4 cups (1 L) total snow peas, broccoli, asparagus pepper 4 Tbsp (60 mL) grated Parmesan cheese	Steam vegetables, add to tomato water and toss with pasta and tomato mixture. Add a little pepper. Sprinkle with Parmesan cheese.

Makes 2 to 4 servings

Linguine with Black Bean Sauce

from *Food to Grow On*

1½ tsp (7 mL) oil

1 small onion, diced fine

→ Sauté until soft.

2 Tbsp (30 mL) fresh ginger, grated

4–6 cloves garlic, minced

1½ tsp (7 mL) sesame oil

→ Add.

1 cup (250 mL) fermented black beans, soaked in boiling water 5 minutes and rinsed twice

→ Process in food processor. Add to above and stir. Add a little water if you want it a bit smoother.

1 Tbsp (15 mL) sugar

½ cup (125 mL) mushroom soy sauce

¼ cup (50 mL) oyster sauce [MSG-free]

¼ cup (50 mL) water

→ Mix until smooth. Cook 3 minutes. Add to above.

1½ lb (750 g) linguine, cooked until al dente

2 cups (500 mL) broccoli florets, blanched

½ cup (125 mL) red pepper, thinly sliced

→ Toss all ingredients together and serve hot.

variation: Feel free to add cooked shrimp or chicken to the pasta, or use whole wheat or spelt pasta.

Add 1 Tbsp (5 mL) jalapeño peppers if a spicy flavour is preferred.

Makes 6 to 8 servings

Spinach Orzo

from *Food to Grow On*

A great way to get kids to eat spinach.

8 cups (2 L) water 2 cups (500 mL) orzo pasta	Boil orzo in water for about 8 minutes or until tender. Set aside.
1 onion 3 cloves garlic, minced 4 tsp (20 mL) olive oil	Sauté onion and garlic in oil in a large saucepan.
1 bunch spinach	Wash spinach and cook until it is completely wilted (it will be a little watery from the steam). Process in blender until smooth.
6 Tbsp (90 mL) grated Parmesan cheese salt and pepper	Toss Parmesan with orzo onion-garlic mixture and spinach. Season to taste with salt and pepper.
4 Tbsp (60 mL) pine nuts, toasted	Sprinkle on top when serving.

Makes 6 to 8 servings

Asian Risotto with Shrimp and Scallops

from The Lazy Gourmet

There's nothing more delicious than perfect homemade risotto. Your guests will love you for it! I always make it at the last moment and let my guests help with the stirring.

6 Tbsp (90 mL) butter	In a sauté pan, melt 2 Tbsp (30 mL) of the butter. Add shiitake mushrooms and sauté for 5 minutes. Set aside.
½ lb (250 g) shiitake mushrooms, cut into strips	
6 cloves garlic, minced	In a large pot, melt the remaining 4 Tbsp (60 mL) of butter and sauté ginger and garlic for a few seconds.
2 cups (500 mL) arborio rice	Add rice and cook for 3 minutes over medium heat.
6½ cups (1.6 L) chicken broth or vegetable stock	
6 Tbsp (90 mL) sherry	Mix together stock, sherry, soy sauce and chili sauce.
2 Tbsp (30 mL) soy sauce	
1 tsp (5 mL) chili sauce	
	Add the mixture, one-third at a time, to the sauté pan, stirring constantly until it is all absorbed. This takes about 20 minutes.
	Make sure to stir the rice continually.
1 small red bell pepper, chopped	Stir in pepper, shrimps and scallops, and simmer for 4 to 5 minutes.
1 lb (500 g) shrimp, deveined and split	
½ lb (250 g) scallops	
½ cup (125 mL) pine nuts	Add pine nuts and sautéed shiitake mushrooms and cook for 1 minute.
1 cup (250 mL) grated Parmesan cheese [Reggianno or Grana Padano]	Stir in grated cheese and serve immediately.

Makes 10 servings

Beef Tenderloin and Asian Noodles

from The Lazy Gourmet

This was a bistro favorite.

4 Tbsp (60 mL) vegetable oil

6–7 oz (170–200 g) tenderloin, cut into thin strips

> Heat the oil in a very hot wok. Stir-fry the tenderloin for 5 minutes.

2 medium red onions, cut into thin strips

½ head napa cabbage, cut into thin strips

2 medium red bell peppers, cut into thin strips

1 lb (500 g) snow peas, cut into strips

> Add the onion, cabbage, red pepper and snow peas. Stir-fry for 1 minute.

2 cups (500 mL) Black Bean Hoisin Sauce [recipe follows]

2 Tbsp (30 mL) sesame oil

8 cups (2 L) cooked Shanghai noodles [available in the refrigerated case of Asian supermarkets]

> Add the Black Bean Hoisin Sauce, sesame oil and Shanghai noodles. Bring the sauce to a boil.

2 green onions, sliced diagonally

> To serve, pile high in a pasta bowl. Garnish with green onions.

Makes 8 servings

Black Bean Hoisin Sauce

½ cup (125 mL) black bean sauce

½ cup (125 mL) soy sauce

½ cup (125 mL) hoisin sauce

¼ cup (50 mL) balsamic vinegar

¼ cup (50 mL) sesame oil

2 Tbsp (30 mL) sugar

> Thoroughly combine all ingredients by hand.

Makes 2 cups (500 mL)

Mee Goreng

from *The Lazy Gourmet*

My mouth waters every time I think of this recipe. Easy to make and really delicious. The fried shallots are a sweet and crispy topping well worth the time they take to make!

3 Tbsp (45 mL) vegetable oil

1½ lb (750 g) snow peas, cut into strips

2 medium red bell peppers, cut into strips

½ head napa cabbage, cut into strips

1 cup (250 mL) extra-firm tofu, fried and cut into strips

Heat oil in a wok over high heat. Sauté snow peas, red pepper, napa cabbage and tofu for 2 minutes.

3 lb (1.4 kg) cooked Shanghai noodles [available in the refrigerated case of Asian supermarkets]

¼ cup (50 mL) water

Add Shanghai noodles and water. Stir-fry for 4 minutes.

½ cup (125 mL) *ketjap manis* [sweet soy sauce, available in the Asian section of supermarkets]

½ cup (125 mL) sweet chili sauce [preferably Yeo brand]

Add *ketjap manis* and sweet chili sauce. Bring the sauce to a boil.

3 cups (750 mL) bean sprouts

Add the bean sprouts and stir-fry for 1 minute.

½ cup (125 mL) sliced green onions

Mound high in a pasta bowl and garnish with green onions and Fried Shallots (recipe follows).

Makes 8 servings

Fried Shallots

8 medium shallots, peeled and sliced

½ cup (125 mL) all-purpose flour

½ cup (125 mL) vegetable oil

Dredge shallots in flour. Heat oil and deep-fry shallots until golden brown and crispy, or until they float. Drain on paper towels.

Makes 8 deep-fried shallots

CHAPTER SIX: PART FOUR

Entrées

Poultry

Grandma Faye's Sticky Apricot Chicken

from The Expo 86 Cookbook

Your guests will call it gourmet; you'll call it easy!

Preheat oven to 375°F (190°C).

one 5-lb (2.5-kg) roasting chicken — Cut chicken into serving-size pieces.

1 cup (250 mL) apricot jam
½ cup (125 mL) chili sauce
¼ cup (50 mL) dry white wine
2 Tbsp (30 mL) soy sauce — Combine and heat, whisking until well blended.
2 Tbsp (30 mL) honey

Place chicken in baking pan. Baste thoroughly with sauce. Bake 1 hour until chicken tests done and surface is sticky.

1 tsp (5 mL) grated fresh ginger
¼ tsp (1 mL) salt

5 oz (150 g) dried apricots — Top with apricots during last half hour of cooking time.

Makes 4 to 6 servings

Pecan Crispy Chicken

from *The Expo 86 Cookbook*

An eighties version of crispy fried chicken. Serve on a bed of wild rice with a steamed vegetable.

Preheat oven to 350°F (180°C).

8 chicken breasts, de-boned — Pound between 2 layers of waxed paper with mallet or cleaver until flat.

½ cup (125 mL) flour
salt and pepper
— Season flour to taste with salt and pepper. Dredge chicken in seasoned flour.

6 Tbsp (90 mL) Dijon mustard
¾ cup (175 mL) butter, melted
2 Tbsp (30 mL) lime juice
1 egg, beaten
— Whisk mustard. Add butter, lime juice and egg. Whisk until well mixed. Dip breasts in sauce.

1½ cups (360 mL) finely chopped pecans
1½ cups (360 mL) fine bread crumbs
— Combine and use to coat chicken pieces. Cover with waxed paper and chill 1 to 2 hours.

Remove waxed paper. Place chicken on baking sheet and bake 35 to 40 minutes.

1 lime, sliced — Place a slice of lime on each piece of chicken.

Makes 6 to 8 servings

Lyla's Cranberry Orange Chicken

from *The Expo 86 Cookbook*

A Friday night special in our home, now on the Lazy Gourmet hit parade!

Preheat oven to 375°F (190°C).

4 lb (2 kg) chicken, cut into serving pieces — Bake 15 minutes, skin side down. Turn.

Sauce

one 14-oz (398-mL) can whole cranberry sauce

¼ cup (50 mL) orange juice concentrate

¼ cup (50 mL) soy sauce

⅓ cup (75 mL) honey

While chicken is baking, combine sauce ingredients in medium saucepan. Bring to a boil, lower heat and let simmer 5 minutes.

tip: You can turn the pieces over every half hour to make sure they are well coated.

Pour sauce over chicken; bake an additional 45 minutes to 1 hour. The longer you bake it, the stickier it will get.

Makes about 6 servings

CHAPTER SIX: PART FIVE

Entrées

Vegetarian

Lazy Gourmet Fettuccine Lasagna

from *The Expo 86 Cookbook*

I first had this recipe at Balducci's in New York City over 30 years ago. It's still a requested item, and my friends love to make it for potluck dinners. It's always a hit!

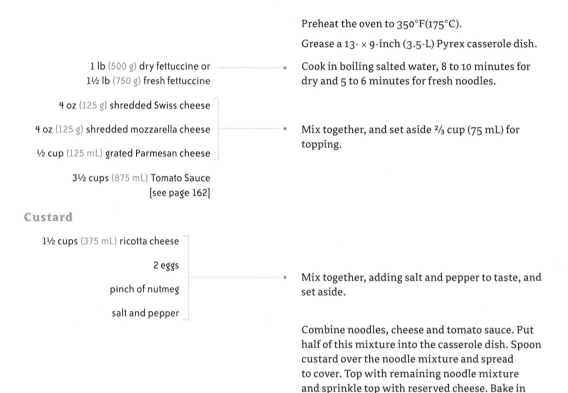

Preheat the oven to 350°F(175°C).

Grease a 13- × 9-inch (3.5-L) Pyrex casserole dish.

1 lb (500 g) dry fettuccine or
1½ lb (750 g) fresh fettuccine

Cook in boiling salted water, 8 to 10 minutes for dry and 5 to 6 minutes for fresh noodles.

4 oz (125 g) shredded Swiss cheese

4 oz (125 g) shredded mozzarella cheese

½ cup (125 mL) grated Parmesan cheese

Mix together, and set aside ⅔ cup (75 mL) for topping.

3½ cups (875 mL) Tomato Sauce [see page 162]

Custard

1½ cups (375 mL) ricotta cheese

2 eggs

pinch of nutmeg

salt and pepper

Mix together, adding salt and pepper to taste, and set aside.

Combine noodles, cheese and tomato sauce. Put half of this mixture into the casserole dish. Spoon custard over the noodle mixture and spread to cover. Top with remaining noodle mixture and sprinkle top with reserved cheese. Bake in preheated oven 35 to 45 minutes until bubbly.

Makes 6 to 8 servings

Broccoli Soufflé

from Mama Never Cooked Like This

Don't be intimidated; this is not a soufflé in the traditional sense. De-lish!

4 cups (1 L) broccoli, cut into small florets and stem pieces

1 small onion, chopped

¼ cup (50 mL) butter

3 Tbsp (45 mL) flour

½ cup (125 mL) water

salt and pepper

3 eggs, beaten

2 cups (500 mL) shredded cheddar cheese

Preheat the oven to 350°F (180°C).

Grease a 9-inch (2.5-L) soufflé dish.

Steam broccoli for 5 minutes. Arrange on bottom of prepared soufflé dish.

Sauté onion in butter until soft.

Add to sautéed onions and stir.

Slowly add water to onions and cook until thickened, stirring constantly. Season to taste with salt and pepper.

Add eggs and cheese last.

Pour over broccoli in soufflé dish and bake in preheated oven for 40 minutes, until firm in the centre.

Makes 8 to 12 servings

Eggplant Moussaka

from *Mama Never Cooked Like This*

2 large eggplants
3 Tbsp (45 mL) oil
salt

→ Cut eggplants into ¼-inch (5-mm) slices, salt both sides, brush with oil and broil until brown.

Tomato Sauce

½ cup (125 mL) chopped onion
½ cup (125 mL) chopped celery
½ cup (125 mL) chopped green pepper
½ cup (125 mL) sliced mushrooms
¼ cup (50 mL) olive oil
one 19-oz (540-mL) tin tomatoes
one 5½-oz (156-mL) tin tomato paste
2 small carrots, grated
1 tsp (5 mL) basil
½ tsp (2 mL) oregano
¼ tsp (1 mL) thyme
2–3 dashes of hot pepper sauce
1 tsp (5 mL) salt
½ tsp (2 mL) pepper

→ Combine ingredients and cook for 20 minutes.

Custard

2 eggs
2 cups (500 mL) cottage cheese
pinch of nutmeg
salt to taste
pepper to taste

→ Mix together.

\>\>

Cheese Mixture

1 cup (250 mL) shredded mozzarella cheese

1 cup (250 mL) shredded Gruyère cheese

⅔ cup (150 mL) grated Parmesan cheese

Mix together.

Preheat the oven to 350°F (180°C).

Grease a 13- × 9-inch (3.5-L) casserole dish.

Layer in prepared casserole dish in the following order: one-third of the tomato sauce, half of the eggplant, all of the custard, half of the cheese mixture, one-third of the tomato sauce, half of the eggplant, one-third of the tomato sauce and half of the cheese mixture.

Bake in preheated oven for 35 to 40 minutes.

Makes 8 servings

Easy Vegetarian Chili

from *Food to Grow On*

A healthful, easy-to-make chili.

1 cup (250 mL) chopped onions 3 cloves garlic, minced 2 Tbsp (30 mL) vegetable oil	Sauté onion and garlic in oil until softened.
1 red pepper, chopped 1 yellow pepper, chopped 1 green pepper, chopped	Add to onion and sauté for 3 minutes.
1 lb (500 g) extra-firm tofu, chopped into pieces one 28-oz (796-mL) can crushed tomatoes one 5½-oz (156-mL) can tomato paste 3 Tbsp (45 mL) chili powder 1 Tbsp (15 mL) dried oregano 1 tsp (5 mL) salt ¼ tsp (1 mL) cayenne	Add to pepper mixture and cook until browned.
¼ tsp (1 mL) freshly ground pepper	Add to tofu and pepper mixture. Bring to a boil. Reduce and simmer for 30 minutes.
one 19-oz (540-mL) can kidney beans, drained one 29-oz (540-mL) can pinto beans, drained 2 cups (500 mL) frozen corn	Add and simmer an additional 30 minutes.

Makes 8 to 10 servings

Easy Broccoli and Tofu Sauté

from *Food to Grow On*

1 Tbsp (15 mL) vegetable oil	Heat in a non-stick skillet.
2 cloves garlic, minced 1 Tbsp (15 mL) grated fresh ginger	Add to oil and sauté for 2 minutes, or until soft.
2 cups (500 mL) broccoli florets	Microwave for 2 minutes on high with ¼ cup (50 mL) of water, and add to ginger and garlic.
2 cups (500 mL) bean sprouts 1 cup (250 mL) sliced carrots	Add to broccoli mixture and sauté 1 minute.
¾ cup (175 mL) vegetable broth 2 Tbsp (30 mL) low-sodium soy sauce 2 Tbsp (30 mL) rice vinegar 1 tsp (5 mL) cornstarch 1 tsp (5 mL) Japanese sesame oil	Combine and stir to dissolve cornstarch. Add to broccoli mixture and cook 1 minute.
¾ lb (375 g) extra-firm tofu, cubed ½ cup (125 mL) celery, sliced on diagonal ½ cup (125 mL) green onions, sliced on diagonal	Add to broccoli mixture, cover and cook for 1 minute. Serve with rice or pasta. **Makes 4 to 6 servings**

Vegetable Fried Rice with Tofu

from Food to Grow On

Always a family favorite. See Uncle Peter's Fried Rice (page 81) for a wheat-free version.

1 cup (250 mL) chopped onion

1 Tbsp (15 mL) grated fresh ginger

2 cloves garlic, minced

2 Tbsp (30 mL) peanut oil

In a wok or skillet, sauté onions, ginger and garlic in oil.

1 cup (250 mL) chopped red cabbage

1 cup (250 mL) thinly sliced carrots

1 cup (250 mL) thinly sliced red peppers

Add and cook until cabbage softens.

3 cups (750 mL) cooked basmati rice

Add to cabbage mixture.

2 Tbsp (30 mL) low-sodium soy sauce

¼ cup (50 mL) vegetable broth

1 Tbsp (15 mL) sherry

1 tsp (5 mL) brown sugar

½ tsp (2 mL) chili paste

½ tsp (2 mL) sesame oil

2 Tbsp (30 mL) oyster sauce

Combine and add to cabbage-and-rice mixture.

¾ cup (175 mL) frozen peas

Heat peas for 1 minute in microwave on high. Add to mixture.

½ lb (250 g) tofu, cubed

Add and heat until tofu is hot.

1–2 eggs [optional]

1 tsp (5 mL) vegetable oil [optional]

Quick-fry eggs in oil in a skillet; then cut into small pieces and add to tofu mixture.

Makes 4 large servings

Spinach Kugel

from *Mama Never Cooked Like This*

We often have this as a starch with our Shabbat dinner. Now I buy whole wheat noodles or spelt noodles and it works really well.

Grease a 13- × 9-inch (3.5-L) baking pan or aluminum ring pan.

one 8-oz (250-g) bunch spinach — Wash and stem, then steam spinach until wilted and rinse with cold water to stop the cooking process.

Chop spinach, or purée in blender or food processor.

12 oz (375 g) egg or spinach fettuccini noodles — Boil until tender.

1 onion, chopped
2–3 Tbsp (30–45 mL) oil — Sauté onion in oil until dark brown and crispy.

Preheat the oven to 350°F (180°C).

5 eggs
1 cup (250 mL) feta cheese, crumbled
½ cup (125 mL) sour cream
2 Tbsp (30 mL) butter, melted — Mix together eggs, cheese, sour cream, butter and seasonings and add spinach and onion.
pinch of nutmeg
Add to noodles.
salt to taste
pepper to taste

Put in prepared pan and bake in preheated oven for 35 to 45 minutes until top is golden.

Makes 8 to 12 servings

Lazy Gourmet's Award-Winning Veggie Burgers

from *The Lazy Gourmet*

When the bistro was open, people used to drive to Vancouver from all over the Lower Mainland for these burgers. It was always so rewarding to hear their stories.

1 lb (500 g) carrots, grated

¾ lb (375 g) cheddar cheese, shredded

¼ cup (50 mL) dried parsley

½ cup (125 mL) soy sauce

2 cups (500 mL) fresh breadcrumbs   Mix together.

5 eggs

1 cup (250 mL) sunflower seeds

1 cup (250 mL) chopped walnuts

8 Kaiser buns   Toast buns.

2 cups (500 mL) Spicy Spinach [recipe follows]

16 slices tomato [optional]

8 slices pickle [optional]

1½ cups (360 mL) Caramelized Onions [recipe follows]   Arrange some Spicy Spinach and, if desired, tomatoes and pickles, on the top half of the buns. Top with Caramelized Onions. Place the burgers on the onions and spread with Chipotle Sauce and Barbecue Sauce. Enjoy!

1 recipe Chipotle Sauce [recipe follows]

1 recipe Barbecue Sauce [recipe follows]

Makes 8 burgers

Spicy Spinach

2 tsp (10 mL) chili oil   In a sauté pan, heat chili oil. Add spinach and cook until wilted.

2 cups (500 mL) baby spinach

Makes 2 cups (500 mL)

>>

Caramelized Onions

2 Tbsp (30 mL) butter

4 medium red onions, thinly sliced

1 Tbsp (15 mL) brown sugar

In a sauté pan, melt butter. Add onions and brown sugar. Cook over low to medium heat, stirring occasionally, until very soft, about 10 minutes.

½ Tbsp (7 mL) red wine vinegar

Add red wine vinegar.

Continue cooking for 5 minutes.

Makes 1½ cups (360 mL)

Chipotle Sauce

1 Tbsp (15 mL) chipotle chilies

½ cup (125 mL) sour cream

juice of ¼ lemon

Place chipotles, sour cream and lemon juice in a food processor or blender and process until smooth.

Makes ½ cup (125 mL)

Barbecue Sauce

2 tsp (10 mL) vegetable oil

1 cup (250 mL) finely chopped onions

In a large pot, heat oil and sauté onions until golden brown, about 10 minutes.

2 cloves garlic, chopped

¾ Tbsp (11 mL) cumin seeds, ground and toasted

1 tsp (5 mL) cayenne pepper

½ cup (125 mL) balsamic vinegar

½ cup (125 mL) red wine vinegar

½ cup (125 mL) soy sauce

⅓ cup (75 mL) brown sugar

½ cup (125 mL) Worcestershire sauce

1 tsp (5 mL) hot pepper sauce

Add to onion.

Simmer until the desired consistency is reached, about 30 minutes. The sauce should be reduced by about two-thirds. Remove from heat. Allow to cool to room temperature.

2 cups (500 mL) ketchup

Add ketchup and blend with a hand blender.

The sauce will keep in the fridge for up to 2 weeks.

Makes 4 cups (1 L)

CHAPTER SEVEN

Muffins, Loaves and More

Ridiculously Simple Banana Bread

from *Mama Never Cooked Like This*

To this day people stop me on the street to tell me how often they make this loaf. When I was having lunch in Balthazar in New York City, the woman at the next table, who was from California, told me that she's famous in her neighbourhood for this recipe.

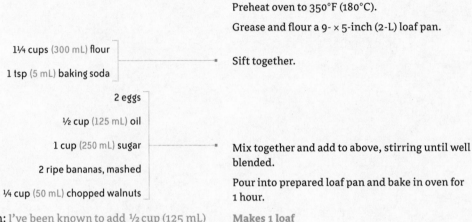

Preheat oven to 350°F (180°C).

Grease and flour a 9- × 5-inch (2-L) loaf pan.

1¼ cups (300 mL) flour

1 tsp (5 mL) baking soda

Sift together.

2 eggs

½ cup (125 mL) oil

1 cup (250 mL) sugar

2 ripe bananas, mashed

¼ cup (50 mL) chopped walnuts

Mix together and add to above, stirring until well blended.

Pour into prepared loaf pan and bake in oven for 1 hour.

Makes 1 loaf

variation: I've been known to add ½ cup (125 mL) mini chocolate chips to the batter before baking.

Melt-In-Your-Mouth Blueberry Muffins

from *Mama Never Cooked Like This*

I like this recipe best in the summer with fresh blueberries.

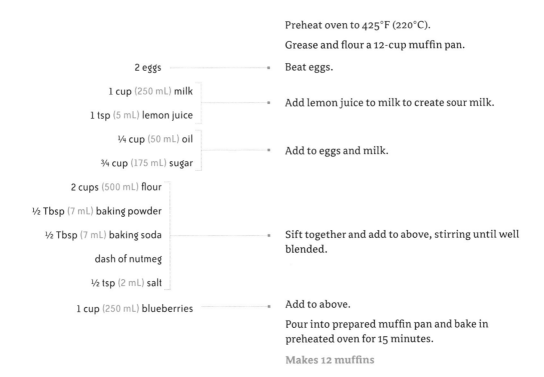

Preheat oven to 425°F (220°C).

Grease and flour a 12-cup muffin pan.

2 eggs · · · · · · · Beat eggs.

1 cup (250 mL) milk
1 tsp (5 mL) lemon juice — Add lemon juice to milk to create sour milk.

¼ cup (50 mL) oil
¾ cup (175 mL) sugar — Add to eggs and milk.

2 cups (500 mL) flour
½ Tbsp (7 mL) baking powder
½ Tbsp (7 mL) baking soda — Sift together and add to above, stirring until well blended.
dash of nutmeg
½ tsp (2 mL) salt

1 cup (250 mL) blueberries · · · Add to above.

Pour into prepared muffin pan and bake in preheated oven for 15 minutes.

Makes 12 muffins

Oatmeal Muffins

from Mama Never Cooked Like This

This is a classic oatmeal muffin. Perfect hot out of the oven on a cold winter's day!

Preheat oven to 400°F (200°C).

Grease and flour a 12-cup muffin pan.

1 cup (250 mL) buttermilk
1 cup (250 mL) quick-cooking rolled oats

Mix together and let stand for 1 hour.

1 egg
½ cup (125 mL) oil
½ cup (125 mL) brown sugar

Mix together and add to above.

1 cup (250 mL) flour
1 tsp (5 mL) baking powder
½ tsp (2 mL) baking soda
½ tsp (2 mL) cinnamon
½ tsp (2 mL) nutmeg
¼–½ tsp (1–2 mL) salt

Sift together and add to above, stirring only until just blended.

½ cup (125 mL) chopped dates [optional]
½ cup (125 mL) chopped walnuts

Add to above.

Pour into prepared muffin pan and bake in preheated oven for 15 to 20 minutes.

Makes 12 muffins

Lemon Loaf

from *Mama Never Cooked Like This*

The fresh lemon juice in the glaze makes all the difference to this loaf. It's a family favorite for special brunches.

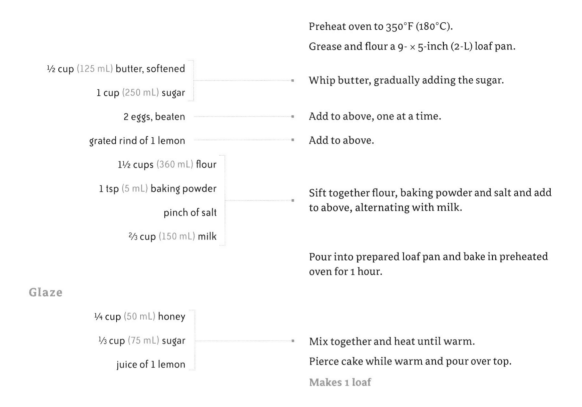

Preheat oven to 350°F (180°C).

Grease and flour a 9- × 5-inch (2-L) loaf pan.

½ cup (125 mL) butter, softened
1 cup (250 mL) sugar

Whip butter, gradually adding the sugar.

2 eggs, beaten

Add to above, one at a time.

grated rind of 1 lemon

Add to above.

1½ cups (360 mL) flour
1 tsp (5 mL) baking powder
pinch of salt
⅔ cup (150 mL) milk

Sift together flour, baking powder and salt and add to above, alternating with milk.

Pour into prepared loaf pan and bake in preheated oven for 1 hour.

Glaze

¼ cup (50 mL) honey
⅓ cup (75 mL) sugar
juice of 1 lemon

Mix together and heat until warm.

Pierce cake while warm and pour over top.

Makes 1 loaf

Cranberry Walnut Bread

from *Mama Never Cooked Like This*

This is a variation from the recipe in *Mama* …. I've replaced the whole wheat flour with spelt flour. I find spelt tastier.

Preheat oven to 375°F (190°C).

Grease and flour a 9- × 5-inch (2-L) loaf pan.

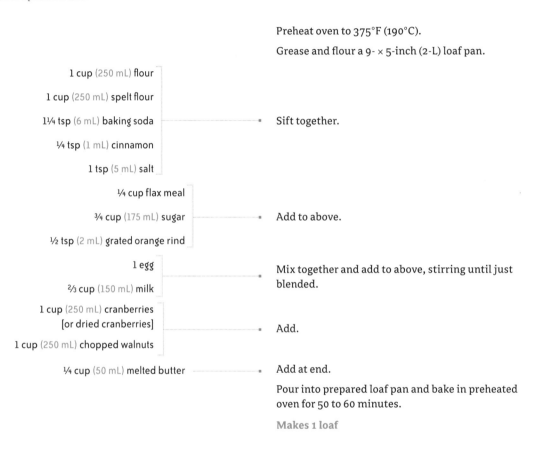

1 cup (250 mL) flour	
1 cup (250 mL) spelt flour	
1¼ tsp (6 mL) baking soda	Sift together.
¼ tsp (1 mL) cinnamon	
1 tsp (5 mL) salt	
¼ cup flax meal	
¾ cup (175 mL) sugar	Add to above.
½ tsp (2 mL) grated orange rind	
1 egg	Mix together and add to above, stirring until just blended.
⅔ cup (150 mL) milk	
1 cup (250 mL) cranberries [or dried cranberries]	Add.
1 cup (250 mL) chopped walnuts	
¼ cup (50 mL) melted butter	Add at end.

Pour into prepared loaf pan and bake in preheated oven for 50 to 60 minutes.

Makes 1 loaf

Black Bottom Muffins

from *Nuts About Chocolate*

This recipe was an all-time favorite in the book co-authored with Deborah Roitberg and one of the few chocolate items included for people allergic to eggs. I've had so many requests for it that I thought it best to republish it now.

Preheat oven to 350°F (180°C).

¼ cup (50 mL) cocoa

½ cup (250 mL) white sugar

1 tsp (5 mL) baking soda

1½ cups (375 mL) flour

Combine in this order.

1 cup (250 mL) water

⅓ cup (75 mL) light oil

2 Tbsp (30 mL) white vinegar

1 tsp (5 mL) vanilla

Mix together until blended, then slowly add to the above.

Line cupcake tins with paper muffin cups and fill each two-thirds full.

½ cup (125 mL) soft cream cheese

1 egg

¼ cup (50 mL) sugar

Blend well and drop by spoonfuls onto chocolate bases.

1 cup (250 mL) mini chocolate chips

Sprinkle each muffin with the chocolate chips.

Bake for 25 minutes or until a toothpick comes out clean.

Makes 12 muffins

Honey Molasses Sweet Bread

from *Mama Never Cooked Like This*

This is a great breakfast bread with cream cheese, or serve it with soup as a main course for lunch or dinner. We always serve it with Bouillabaisse (see page 114). It's the perfect marriage!

Preheat oven to 350°F (180°C).

Grease and flour a 9- × 5-inch (2-L) loaf pan.

1 cup (250 mL) milk

½ cup (125 mL) honey

½ cup (125 mL) molasses

Cook milk, honey and molasses on low heat, stirring until blended.

Remove from heat and let cool slightly.

2 eggs

¼ cup (50 mL) soft butter

Beat eggs and butter.

Then add to milk mixture and beat.

2½ cups (625 mL) whole wheat flour

1 Tbsp (15 mL) baking powder

1 tsp (5 mL) salt

Sift together flour, salt and baking powder, then mix into above.

Pour into prepared pan and bake in preheated oven for 1 hour. Cool before slicing.

Makes 1 loaf

My Favorite Bran Muffins

from *Let Me in the Kitchen*

Kids have a great time making this recipe. It's easy and the results are consistently good.

Preheat the oven to 425°F (220°C).

Grease and flour a 12-cup muffin pan.

1 egg — Break egg into a large bowl and beat with a whisk.

⅓ cup (75 mL) white sugar
⅓ cup (75 mL) brown sugar — Add both white and brown sugar and mix well.

⅓ cup (75 mL) vegetable oil — Add oil and mix thoroughly.

1 cup (250 mL) mashed ripe bananas and/or buttermilk — Add mashed bananas and/or buttermilk. You can use both as long as the total amount is 1 cup (250 mL).

1 cup (250 mL) flour
1 tsp (5 mL) baking soda
1 tsp (5 mL) baking powder — Sift flour, baking soda and baking powder into the bowl. Mix until everything is well blended.

1 cup (250 mL) natural bran
1 tsp (5 mL) pure vanilla extract
⅓ cup (75 mL) raisins
⅓ cup (75 mL) walnut pieces — Add bran, vanilla, raisins and walnuts and mix.

Fill muffin pan cups two-thirds full of batter. Bake in preheated oven for 25 minutes. Let cool a few minutes before eating.

Makes 12 muffins

Raspberry-Blueberry Cornmeal Muffins

from The Expo 86 Cookbook

Feel free to use any summer fruit like peaches, nectarines or blackberries. Have fun!

Preheat oven to 400°F (200°C).
Grease and flour a 12-cup muffin pan.

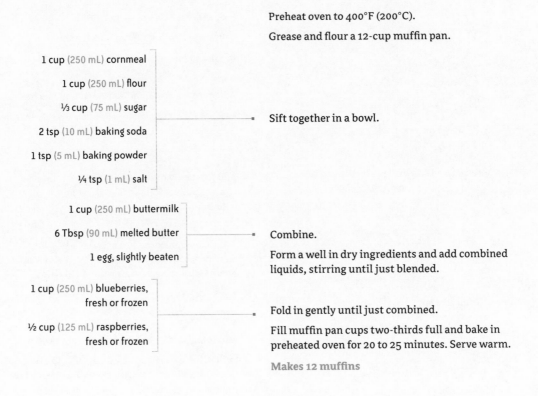

1 cup (250 mL) cornmeal
1 cup (250 mL) flour
⅓ cup (75 mL) sugar
2 tsp (10 mL) baking soda
1 tsp (5 mL) baking powder
¼ tsp (1 mL) salt

Sift together in a bowl.

1 cup (250 mL) buttermilk
6 Tbsp (90 mL) melted butter
1 egg, slightly beaten

Combine.

Form a well in dry ingredients and add combined liquids, stirring until just blended.

1 cup (250 mL) blueberries, fresh or frozen
½ cup (125 mL) raspberries, fresh or frozen

Fold in gently until just combined.

Fill muffin pan cups two-thirds full and bake in preheated oven for 20 to 25 minutes. Serve warm.

Makes 12 muffins

Sticky Cinnamon Buns

from *The Expo 86 Cookbook*

The sticky bun of the century! Definitely worth the effort.

½ cup (125 mL) warm milk
1 tsp (10 mL) sugar
1 pkg. dry yeast

Dissolve sugar in milk. Add yeast and let stand 10 minutes.

1 cup (250 mL) butter
½ cup (125 mL) sugar

Using electric mixer and large bowl, cream butter. Add sugar, creaming until smooth.

3 eggs

Add eggs one at a time, mixing well after each addition.

¾ cup (175 mL) milk
½ tsp (2 mL) salt

Add to above.

Stir in yeast mixture.

3 cups (750 mL) flour

Using low speed of mixer, beat in flour until well blended.

2 cups (500 mL) flour

Add until dough is very stiff and you can no longer use mixer.

Now add enough flour so that dough does not stick to your hands. Form a ball. Place dough in lightly oiled bowl, turning to coat all sides. Cover with oiled waxed paper and a damp towel. Let rise in a warm place until doubled (about 2 hours). Punch down and roll out into a large rectangle.

½ cup (125 mL) butter, melted

Brush dough with butter.

¾ cup (175 mL) sugar
¼ cup (50 mL) cinnamon [yes!]
1 cup (250 mL) raisins [optional]

Mix together sugar and cinnamon.

Sprinkle dough with sugar-cinnamon mixture and raisins if desired.

Roll up dough lengthwise and cut into 2-inch (5-cm) rounds.

Lightly grease two 9-inch (1.5-L) round baking pans.

½ cup (125 mL) butter, melted
¾ cup (175 mL) brown sugar
¼ cup (50 mL) honey
1 cup (250 mL) walnut or pecan pieces

Mix together and spread over bottom of prepared pans. Place rounds on top, cover with oiled waxed paper and let rise an additional 30 minutes.

Preheat oven to 375°F (190°C).

Bake for 25 to 30 minutes. Let sit a few minutes before inverting onto a plate.

Makes 12 to 18 buns

Food Processor Challah

from *The Expo 86 Cookbook*

A soft and sweet egg bread traditionally served on Friday evenings in Jewish homes. Your family and friends will be impressed with this beautiful, easy-to-make challah.

1 pkg. dry yeast
1 tsp (5 mL) sugar
1 cup (250 mL) warm water

Combine thoroughly and let sit 10 minutes.

3 cups (750 mL) flour
⅓ cup (75 mL) sugar
½ tsp (2 mL) salt

Place in food processor bowl and use on/off to process.

1 egg
¼ cup (50 mL) oil

With machine running, add egg, oil and yeast mixture. Process until a ball forms (about 1 minute).

Turn onto floured surface and knead 1 minute. Place in lightly oiled bowl, turning to coat all sides. Cover with lightly oiled waxed paper and a damp towel. Let rise in a warm place 2 hours until doubled in volume.

Punch down. Divide two-thirds of dough into one ball and remainder into another. Divide larger ball into 3 pieces. Knead each for a few minutes, then roll each into a rope and braid the 3 together. Repeat with smaller ball. Top the larger braid with the smaller one and place on a lightly oiled baking sheet. Cover with a damp towel and let rise in a warm place for 1 hour until doubled.

Preheat the oven to 375°F (190°C).

1 egg, beaten
3 Tbsp (45 mL) sesame seeds

Brush dough with egg and sprinkle with seeds.

Bake in preheated oven for 35 to 40 minutes until golden brown. When done, the bottom should make a hollow sound when tapped.

Makes 1 large loaf

Grandma's Sour Cream Coffee Cake

Preheat oven to 350°F (180°C).

Grease and flour a 9-inch (3-L) tube pan. You can also use a 9-inch (2.5-L) springform pan, in which case no preparation is necessary.

1 cup (250 mL) butter, softened — Cream.

1½ cups (360 mL) sugar — Add gradually to butter.

3 eggs — Add eggs, one at a time, mixing well after each addition. Set aside.

1½ cups (360 mL) sour cream
1 tsp (5 mL) vanilla extract
1 tsp (5 mL) baking soda

Mix together and set aside.

3 cups (750 mL) flour
2 tsp (10 mL) baking powder
½ tsp (2 mL) salt

Sift well.

Alternately add flour mixture and sour cream mixture to butter mixture, starting and ending with the flour.

Place half the batter in prepared pan.

Centre and Topping

1 cup (250 mL) brown sugar
1 Tbsp (15 mL) cinnamon
¾ cup (175 mL) walnuts or pecans, chopped
2 Tbsp (30 mL) butter, melted

Mix all ingredients together.

Sprinkle cake with half the cinnamon-nut mixture. Cover with rest of batter. Sprinkle with remainder of mixture.

Bake in preheated oven for 50 to 60 minutes until done.

Makes 8 to 10 servings

variation: Try adding ½ cup (125 mL) of mini chocolate chips to the centre and topping mixture. My sister Lynn makes it this way for her kids' special birthday cakes.

High-Fibre Banana Bread

Everyone is amazed that this banana bread tastes so good, despite having less than half the oil of my famous Ridiculously Simple Banana Bread (see page 172). (And way more fibre!)

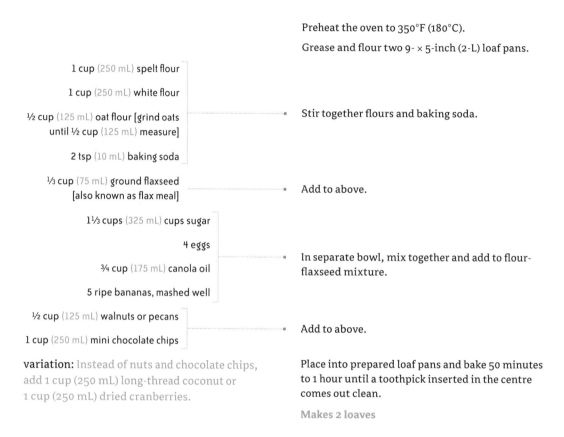

Preheat the oven to 350°F (180°C).

Grease and flour two 9- × 5-inch (2-L) loaf pans.

1 cup (250 mL) spelt flour

1 cup (250 mL) white flour

½ cup (125 mL) oat flour [grind oats until ½ cup (125 mL) measure]

2 tsp (10 mL) baking soda

Stir together flours and baking soda.

⅓ cup (75 mL) ground flaxseed [also known as flax meal]

Add to above.

1⅓ cups (325 mL) cups sugar

4 eggs

¾ cup (175 mL) canola oil

5 ripe bananas, mashed well

In separate bowl, mix together and add to flour-flaxseed mixture.

½ cup (125 mL) walnuts or pecans

1 cup (250 mL) mini chocolate chips

Add to above.

variation: Instead of nuts and chocolate chips, add 1 cup (250 mL) long-thread coconut or 1 cup (250 mL) dried cranberries.

Place into prepared loaf pans and bake 50 minutes to 1 hour until a toothpick inserted in the centre comes out clean.

Makes 2 loaves

Blueberry Oatmeal Muffins

These are my family's favorite summer muffins.

Preheat the oven to 400°F (200°C).

Lightly grease and flour a 12-cup muffin pan.

1 cup (250 mL) quick oats

1 cup (250 mL) buttermilk

Mix oats and buttermilk together, and let stand for 10 minutes.

¼ cup (50 mL) butter, melted

1 egg

½ tsp (2 mL) vanilla extract

Add melted butter, egg and vanilla and blend well.

½ cup (175 mL) flour

½ cup (175 mL) spelt flour

1 tsp (5 mL) baking powder

½ tsp (2 mL) baking soda

½ tsp (2 mL) salt

3 Tbsp (45 mL) flaxseed

Sift together flours, baking soda, baking powder and salt, then add to liquid mixture with flaxseed and mix until just blended.

Do not overbeat.

1½ cups (360 mL) fresh blueberries

Fold in blueberries. Fill muffin pan cups two-thirds full of batter.

Streusel Topping

2 Tbsp (30 mL) brown sugar

2 tsp (10 mL) melted butter

½ tsp (2 mL) cinnamon

Mix brown sugar, melted butter and cinnamon. Sprinkle topping on muffins.

Bake in preheated oven for 18 to 20 minutes until a toothpick inserted in muffins comes out clean.

Makes 12 muffins

tip: It's okay if there's blueberry juice on the toothpick, as these healthful muffins are filled with lots of blueberries.

Homemade Waffles

This variation of the recipe in my kids' cookbook is easier to make and always a hit served with fresh berries and cream or yogurt. For variety, I've added toasted or candied pecans to the mixture and served the waffles with fresh peaches and warmed maple syrup. Yum!

This recipe can also be used for pancakes.

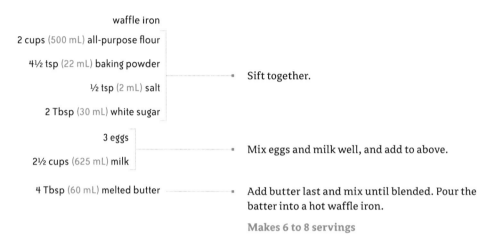

waffle iron

2 cups (500 mL) all-purpose flour

4½ tsp (22 mL) baking powder

½ tsp (2 mL) salt   Sift together.

2 Tbsp (30 mL) white sugar

3 eggs

2½ cups (625 mL) milk   Mix eggs and milk well, and add to above.

4 Tbsp (60 mL) melted butter   Add butter last and mix until blended. Pour the batter into a hot waffle iron.

Makes 6 to 8 servings

Lazy Gourmet Granola

This is the granola we at The Lazy Gourmet send out daily with catered breakfasts.

Preheat oven to 325°F (160°C).

1 cup (250 mL) butter
½ cup (125 mL) brown sugar
½ cup (125 mL) corn syrup
dash of vanilla extract

Heat until butter melts.

4 cups (1 L) oats
¼ tsp (1 mL) salt
1 cup (250 mL) coconut
1 cup (250 mL) pumpkin seeds
1 cup (250 mL) almonds
1 cup (250 mL) sunflower seeds
1 cup (250 mL) cashews

Mix together. Add butter mixture.

Spread out on a baking sheet and bake in preheated oven for 45 minutes to 1 hour. Stir every 15 minutes or so.

Remove from oven and cool.

1 cup (250 mL) raisins
1 cup (250 mL) dried cranberries

Add to cooled baked mixture.

Makes 10 cups (2.5 L)

CHAPTER EIGHT

Desserts

Famous Lemon Cheesecake

from Mama Never Cooked Like This

A classic recipe that I developed over 30 years ago for my dear friend Larry Lillo, who loved cheesecake!

Preheat oven to 350°F (180°C).

Crust

1⅓ cups (325 mL) graham cracker crumbs

⅓ cup (75 mL) butter

¼ cup (50 mL) brown sugar

Mix together and press into the bottom of a 9-inch (23-cm) springform pan.

Bake in preheated oven for 5 minutes.

Leave oven on.

Filling

1 lb (500 g) spreadable cream cheese

3 medium eggs

½ cup (125 mL) sour cream

⅔ cup (150 mL) sugar

2 Tbsp (30 mL) lemon juice

Mix together well to form a batter.

Pour over crust.

Bake in oven for 30 to 35 minutes until firm to the touch.

Leave oven on.

Topping

1 cup (250 mL) sour cream

4 Tbsp (60 mL) sugar

2 Tbsp (30 mL) lemon juice

Mix together and spread over cheesecake.

Return to oven for 5 minutes.

Makes 10 servings

Strawberry Meringue Torte

from Mama Never Cooked Like This

This is the perfect dessert to serve guests who have wheat allergies! It's so easy to prepare, too.

Preheat oven to 400°F (200°C).

Line baking sheets with waxed paper on which three 9-inch (23-cm) circles have been traced.

Meringue (make the night before)

8 egg whites

½ tsp (2 mL) cream of tartar

dash of salt

Beat until stiff.

1½ cups (350 mL) sugar

Slowly add sugar, continuing to beat until egg whites are stiff and glossy.

Spread over circles on paper.

Place baking sheets in oven. Turn oven off and leave in overnight.

Chocolate

10 oz (300 g) semi-sweet chocolate

Melt chocolate over hot water. Do not allow water to boil.

½ cup (125 mL) whipping cream

Add cream to chocolate and let sit.

Cream

4 cups (1 L) whipping cream

½ cup (125 mL) icing sugar

2 tsp (10 mL) Cointreau [or kirsch]

Whip until stiff, slowly adding icing sugar and Cointreau or kirsch.

Strawberries

4 cups (1 L) strawberries

Slice strawberries. Save the larger ones for decoration.

Place first meringue on dish.

Spread half of chocolate over meringue, then add quarter of cream, half of strawberries, another layer of meringue, rest of chocolate, quarter of cream and rest of sliced strawberries. Finish with last meringue.

Ice cake with remaining cream and decorate with larger strawberries.

Makes 10 to 12 servings

Valentine's Day Carrot Cake

from Let Me in the Kitchen

This is still my favorite carrot cake!

Preheat the oven to 300°F (150°C).

Grease 1 round 8-inch (20-cm) cake pan and 1 square 8-inch (20-cm) cake pan, and line bottom of each pan with parchment paper.

2 cups (500 mL) grated carrots

½ cup (125 mL) walnut pieces

Add nuts to carrots. Set aside.

1½ cups (360 mL) white flour

2 tsp (10 mL) baking powder

2 tsp (10 mL) baking soda

2 tsp (10 mL) cinnamon

Sift flour with baking powder, baking soda and cinnamon into a small bowl and set aside.

3 eggs

Use an electric mixer to beat eggs in a large bowl until light and fluffy.

1 cup (250 mL) white sugar

Slowly pour in sugar while beating.

1 cup (250 mL) vegetable oil

Then slowly pour in oil while the mixer is on high speed.

Add flour mixture to egg mixture and blend slowly. Add carrots and walnuts and blend.

Pour half of cake mix into each prepared pan. Bake for 1 hour.

When cakes are cool, remove from the pans and cut the round layer down the centre. Fit the two halves of the round cake onto adjacent sides of the square cake to create a heart shape. Instant magic!

Ice with Cream Cheese Icing (recipe follows).

Serves 8 to 12

Cream Cheese Icing

1½ cups (360 mL) spreadable cream cheese

½ cup (125 mL) butter, softened

1 cup (250 mL) icing sugar

1 tsp (5 mL) vanilla extract

Use an electric mixer on high speed to beat all ingredients in a bowl until smooth. If icing is too thick, add a little milk.

tip: Use your judgment as to how much sweetness you would like in the icing.

Mesclun Greens with Red Pepper,
Chèvre and Macadamia Nuts   **p. 64**

Cream of Broccoli Soup   p. 38

Cold Beet Soup

p. 40

Roasted Red Pepper Soup

p. 44

Camembert-en-Croûte p. 13

Toasted Coconut Prawns with
Sun-Dried Cherry Chutney   **p. 31**

Lazy Gourmet Granola p. 187

Chocolate Truffle Cookies   p. 245

Skor Bar Cake   p. 216

Ridiculously Simple Banana Bread   p. 172
and High-Fibre Banana Bread   p. 184

Double Chocolate Frangelico Cheesecake

from *The Expo 86 Cookbook*

Preheat oven to 350°F (180°C).

Chocolate Crumb Crust

⅔ box chocolate wafers, processed into crumbs

⅓ cup (75 mL) butter, melted

Mix crumbs and butter together and press into bottom and sides of a 10-inch (3-L) springform pan. Bake 6 minutes, then remove from oven.

Leave oven on.

1 lb (500 g) spreadable cream cheese

½ cup (125 mL) sugar

9 oz (300 g) semi-sweet chocolate, melted

⅔ cup (150 mL) sour cream

3 eggs

2 Tbsp (30 mL) Frangelico liqueur

¼ cup (50 mL) hazelnut butter [or Nutella]

Combine and beat with electric mixer on medium-high speed 5 to 6 minutes until light and creamy.

Pour over crust and bake in preheated oven for 40 to 45 minutes until firm to the touch.

Cool, then chill in the refrigerator.

Cream Topping

1 cup (250 mL) whipping cream

2–3 Tbsp (30–45 mL) icing sugar

Whip cream with sugar until thick.

2 Tbsp (30 mL) Frangelico liqueur

Add liqueur.

Spread over cake.

Makes 12 servings

tip: If you can find a good Swiss hazelnut fondant called *gianduja*, top the cake with curls of this fabulous treat. (A vegetable peeler does the trick.)

Festive Sherry Trifle

from *The Expo 86 Cookbook*

This is a great recipe year-round, and even more special at holiday time. Don't be put off by the number of steps in this recipe. It's really easy and fun to make, perfect for special occasions.

Preheat oven to 375°F (190°C).

Line a jelly roll pan with waxed paper.

Sponge Cake

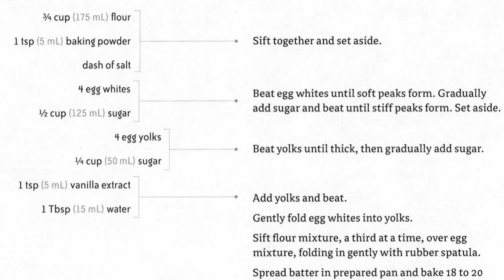

¾ cup (175 mL) flour

1 tsp (5 mL) baking powder

dash of salt

Sift together and set aside.

4 egg whites

½ cup (125 mL) sugar

Beat egg whites until soft peaks form. Gradually add sugar and beat until stiff peaks form. Set aside.

4 egg yolks

¼ cup (50 mL) sugar

Beat yolks until thick, then gradually add sugar.

1 tsp (5 mL) vanilla extract

1 Tbsp (15 mL) water

Add yolks and beat.

Gently fold egg whites into yolks.

Sift flour mixture, a third at a time, over egg mixture, folding in gently with rubber spatula.

Spread batter in prepared pan and bake 18 to 20 minutes. When cool, break into pieces.

>>

Easy Crème Pâtissière

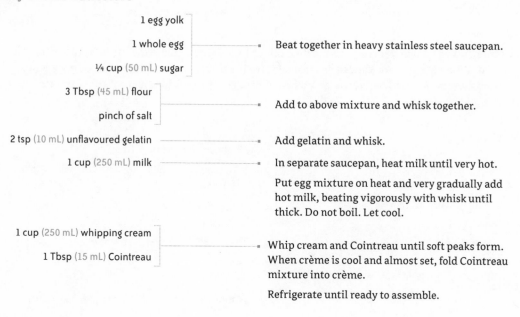

1 egg yolk
1 whole egg
¼ cup (50 mL) sugar

Beat together in heavy stainless steel saucepan.

3 Tbsp (45 mL) flour
pinch of salt

Add to above mixture and whisk together.

2 tsp (10 mL) unflavoured gelatin

Add gelatin and whisk.

1 cup (250 mL) milk

In separate saucepan, heat milk until very hot.

Put egg mixture on heat and very gradually add hot milk, beating vigorously with whisk until thick. Do not boil. Let cool.

1 cup (250 mL) whipping cream
1 Tbsp (15 mL) Cointreau

Whip cream and Cointreau until soft peaks form. When crème is cool and almost set, fold Cointreau mixture into crème.

Refrigerate until ready to assemble.

Whipped Cream

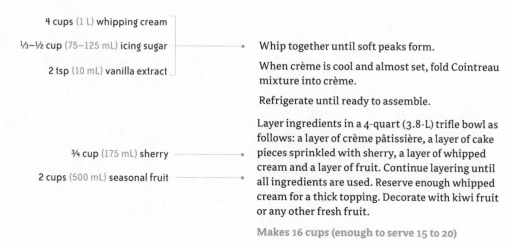

4 cups (1 L) whipping cream
⅓–½ cup (75–125 mL) icing sugar
2 tsp (10 mL) vanilla extract

Whip together until soft peaks form.

When crème is cool and almost set, fold Cointreau mixture into crème.

Refrigerate until ready to assemble.

¾ cup (175 mL) sherry
2 cups (500 mL) seasonal fruit

Layer ingredients in a 4-quart (3.8-L) trifle bowl as follows: a layer of crème pâtissière, a layer of cake pieces sprinkled with sherry, a layer of whipped cream and a layer of fruit. Continue layering until all ingredients are used. Reserve enough whipped cream for a thick topping. Decorate with kiwi fruit or any other fresh fruit.

Makes 16 cups (enough to serve 15 to 20)

Marie-Lore's Dacquoise

from *The Expo 86 Cookbook*

Once there was a Vancouver restaurant called Lili La Puce, which made the most fabulous torte in the world. When Marie-Lore Rhodes generously gave me this recipe and I made it for my friends, they were convinced that I had resurrected a memory. This torte is for lovers of the ultimate in gastronomic treats!

Meringue

Preheat oven to 250°F (120°C).

Cover a 10- × 12-inch (25- × 30-cm) baking sheet with waxed paper.

6 egg whites, at room temperature

dash of salt

¼ tsp (1 mL) cream of tartar

1 tsp (5 mL) vanilla extract

Beat together until soft peaks form.

1 cup (250 mL) sugar

Gradually add sugar, 1 Tbsp (15 mL) at a time.

1½ cups (360 mL) toasted hazelnuts or almonds, ground

4½ tsp (22 mL) cornstarch

Mix nuts and cornstarch and fold into egg white mixture, in thirds, until blended.

Spread on prepared baking sheet. Bake 1½ hours until crisp. Turn off the heat and leave in oven another ½ hour.

Cut into thirds.

Buttercream

6 egg yolks

6 Tbsp (90 mL) sugar

2 tsp (10 mL) vanilla extract

Place in food processor or blender and blend for 10 seconds.

2 cups (500 mL) unsalted butter, softened

Keep machine running and gradually add softened butter.

¼ cup (50 mL) unsweetened cocoa powder

2 tsp (10 mL) instant coffee

2 Tbsp (30 mL) coffee liqueur

Add to egg yolk mixture, mixing until smooth.

Spread meringue layers with buttercream and chill until firm.

\>\>

Topping

2 Tbsp (30 mL) icing sugar ⸺ ▪ To garnish, sprinkle icing sugar over top of cake.

1 cup (250 mL) whipping cream, whipped ⸺ ▪ Spread cream over sides.

½ cup (125 mL) toasted almonds, sliced ⸺ ▪ Press nuts into cream.

Makes 8 to 10 servings

Triple Berry Crisp Pie

from *The Expo 86 Cookbook*

When *The Expo 86 Cookbook* was created in 1986, this was our photographer Derik Murray's favorite pie! Because this recipe is also good with frozen fruit, it's a year-round favorite.

▪ Preheat oven to 375°F (190°C).

one 9-inch (23-cm) deep dish pie crust [see No-Fail Pastry, page 208], pre-baked 7 to 9 minutes at 375°F (190°C)

1 cup (250 mL) strawberries or peaches

2 cups (500 mL) fresh or frozen raspberries

3 cups (750 mL) fresh or frozen blueberries

1 cup (250 mL) sugar

3 Tbsp (45 mL) cornstarch

¼ tsp (1 mL) nutmeg

▪ Mix filling ingredients together in large bowl. Pour into pre-baked pie crust.

Topping

¾ cup (175 mL) flour

1 cup (250 mL) brown sugar

½ cup (125 mL) quick-cooking oats

½ cup (125 mL) cold butter

▪ Rub together to form crumbs.

Spread topping over berries.

Place pie on baking sheet (to catch runover juice) and bake in preheated oven for 40 minutes.

Makes 8 servings

Chocolate Pecan Pie

from The Expo 86 Cookbook

We used to wholesale this pie to a number of local restaurants. It became their signature dessert. Now we only make it on special occasions. It's the perfect combination of nuts and chocolate.

Preheat oven to 375°F (190°C).

Place a circle of parchment paper in the bottom of a 9- or 10-inch (23- or 25-cm) pie plate.

Chocolate Pastry

1 cup (250 mL) flour

¼ cup (50 mL) brown sugar — Combine in a bowl.

3 Tbsp (45 mL) cocoa powder

½ cup (125 mL) cold butter, cubed — Blend into flour mixture until coarse, using pastry blender, 2 knives or a food processor.

2 Tbsp (30 mL) milk

1 tsp (5 mL) vanilla extract — Add to mixture and combine until just blended.

Pat dough into prepared pie plate and crimp edges.

Filling

3 eggs — Beat well.

1 cup (250 mL) brown sugar — Stir into eggs.

⅓ cup (75 mL) butter, melted

½ tsp (2 mL) vanilla extract — Stir into eggs-sugar mixture.

1 cup (250 mL) pecan halves, toasted — Spread pecans in bottom of pie shell.

Pour filling over pecans.

Bake 15 minutes, then reduce heat to 350°F (180°C), and bake an additional 30 minutes. Let cool to room temperature.

Fudge Glaze

2 Tbsp (30 mL) butter — Melt over hot water.

1 cup (250 mL) chocolate chips or
6 oz (175 g) semi-sweet chocolate, chopped — Add to pan of melted butter; melt, then cool slightly.

2 Tbsp (30 mL) brandy — Gently stir into butter-chocolate mixture.

Spread glaze over pie.

Makes 8 servings

Double Fudge Chocolate Cake

from *The Expo 86 Cookbook*

Thanks to my friend Roberta Niemann for sharing this recipe with me. It has been the Lazy Gourmet standard chocolate cake for over 25 years.

Preheat oven to 350°F (180°C).

Grease and flour two 8- or 9-inch (1.2- or 1.5-L) round cake pans.

2 eggs

1 cup (250 mL) sugar

2 Tbsp (30 mL) butter, softened

1 cup (250 mL) light oil

½ cup (125 mL) cocoa powder, packed

½ cup (125 mL) buttermilk

1 tsp (5 mL) vanilla extract

In a large bowl, add ingredients one at a time in order listed, beating after each addition.

2¼ cups (550 mL) flour

1½ tsp (7 mL) baking soda

1½ tsp (7 mL) baking powder

In separate bowl, sift together, then add to above.

1 cup (250 mL) boiling water

Fold into above.

½ cup (125 mL) chocolate chips

Add to above and mix in.

Place mixture in prepared pans. Bake for 25 minutes.

Ice with Incredible Chocolate Icing (recipe follows).

Makes 10 to 12 servings

Incredible Chocolate Icing

1 cup (250 mL) butter, softened

¼ cup (50 mL) hot water or hot coffee

2 cups (500 mL) icing sugar

1⅓ cups (325 mL) cocoa powder

Place in a blender or food processor and blend for a few seconds.

¼ cup (50 mL) milk

2 tsp (10 mL) vanilla extract

Add liquids and blend until smooth. For a thinner icing, use additional milk.

Makes approximately 3 cups

Ron Lammie's White Chocolate Mousse

from The Expo 86 Cookbook

Ron Lammie worked at a number of restaurants in Vancouver in the eighties. When I put together *The Expo 86 Cookbook*, I took the opportunity to ask him for this coveted recipe.

White Chocolate Layer

12 oz (375 g) white chocolate	Chop into small pieces and melt over hot water. Cool.
3 cups (750 mL) whipping cream	Whip until stiff, then refrigerate 4 to 6 hours or overnight.
2 egg yolks 2 whole eggs	Beat egg yolks and whole eggs together.
¾ cup (175 mL) sugar	Add sugar and beat until a light lemon colour.
1½ Tbsp (22 mL) unflavoured gelatin	Stir a little of the egg mixture into the gelatin, then add gelatin to eggs and mix thoroughly.
	Beat melted chocolate slowly into mixture.
	Fold in whipped cream. Place in 8-cup (2-L) mould and refrigerate for 2 hours.

Dark Chocolate Layer

24 oz (750 g) semi-sweet chocolate	Chop into small bits.
1½ cups (360 mL) whipping cream ⅓ cup (75 mL) sugar 3 Tbsp (45 mL) butter	Combine and bring to a boil. Remove from heat. Add chocolate and mix until blended.
	Cool at room temperature for 2 hours.
2 Tbsp (30 mL) Grand Marnier	Add Grand Marnier to chocolate-and-cream mixture. Pour over top of white chocolate mould. Refrigerate 3 hours.
	Dip mould in warm water. Turn onto serving dish.

Makes 8 to 10 servings

Crème Brulée

from The Lazy Gourmet

I recently bought my first torch for use at home. My guests have fun coming into the kitchen to help with torching the sugar.

Preheat oven to 350°F (180°C).

2 cups (500 mL) whipping cream

⅓ cup (75 mL) granulated sugar

½ vanilla bean [split lengthwise]

Combine the cream, granulated sugar and vanilla bean in a saucepan and bring to a boil. Cool slightly. Discard the vanilla bean.

4 egg yolks

Beat the egg yolks together. Slowly add the hot cream to the yolks, beating vigorously with a whisk. Pour the mixture through a fine sieve.

Pour into 4 individual glass or porcelain ramekins (approximately 5-oz | 150-g). Place the ramekins in a shallow baking pan. Fill the pan with water until it reaches halfway up the sides of the ramekins. Cover the pan with aluminum foil.

Bake for 1 hour, or until the custards are set but still jiggle in the middle. Cool on a rack, then remove from the pan and refrigerate for at least 1 hour, until chilled.

1 Tbsp (15 mL) brown sugar

9 Tbsp (135 mL) granulated sugar

To serve, combine brown sugar and granulated sugar and sprinkle evenly over the surface of the custards. Brown evenly with a blowtorch or under the broiler. Be sure to only brown (caramelize) the sugar, not burn it.

Makes 4 servings

substitution: Different liqueurs can be used to alter the flavour. For example: in place of the vanilla bean, use 1 Tbsp (15 mL) of your favorite liqueur.

Lazy Gourmet's Lava Cakes

from *The Lazy Gourmet*

Roy's Restaurants, with 33 locations worldwide, specialize in Hawaiian Fusion cuisine. The first Roy's was opened by Roy Yamaguchi in Honolulu in 1988. When my husband and I go to Hawaii we always have Roy's Melting Hot Chocolate Soufflés at least once. This recipe was given to me by Hawaiian friends who promised that it would enable me to replicate this stupendous dessert.

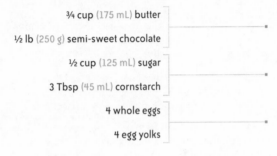

¾ cup (175 mL) butter

½ lb (250 g) semi-sweet chocolate

Melt butter and chocolate in a saucepan over low heat.

½ cup (125 mL) sugar

3 Tbsp (45 mL) cornstarch

Mix sugar and cornstarch together in a bowl.

4 whole eggs

4 egg yolks

Crack eggs into another bowl and whisk yolks into whole eggs.

When chocolate has melted, remove from heat. Whisk in sugar-cornstarch mixture until blended. Add eggs and stir until smooth. Chill in the fridge overnight.

Preheat the oven to 400°F (200°C).

Line a baking sheet with parchment paper.

Line 8 metal rings (you can use 1½-inch/3.8-cm deep tin cans with both ends opened) with a strip of parchment paper, or grease ½-cup (120-mL) ramekins. Set the rings on the baking sheet and brush generously with butter. Scoop chocolate filling into each one, filling them two-thirds full.

Bake in preheated oven for 12 to 15 minutes.

Remove from oven. Slide a metal spatula under cakes and transfer to serving plates. Gently slide the rings off cakes and remove the parchment. Dust with icing sugar and serve immediately.

Makes 8 servings

Macadamia and Coconut Tarte

from *The Lazy Gourmet*

I truly dream about this recipe. If you like butter tarts, you're in for a treat!

	Preheat the oven to 325°F (160°C).
	Grease a 9-inch (23-cm) tart pan and line the bottom with a circle of parchment paper.
½ recipe Sweet Dough [see page 205]	On a floured surface, roll dough into a circle ⅛ inch (3 mm) thick. Fit pastry into the pan, trimming the excess away with a sharp knife. Line the shell with a piece of foil and weigh it down with some grain or beans. Bake the shell until slightly golden, 12 to 15 minutes.
	Remove the foil and grain or beans.
	Increase the oven temperature to 350°F (180°C).
½ cup (125 mL) flaked unsweetened coconut	On a baking sheet, toast coconut until golden brown, 5 to 7 minutes. Stir occasionally for even toasting. Set aside.
1 cup (250 mL) macadamia nuts	On a separate baking sheet, toast the macadamia nuts until golden brown, 6 to 8 minutes. Cool. Chop very coarsely into ¼-inch (5-mm) chunks and set aside.
	Increase the oven temperature to 375°F (190°C).
6 Tbsp (90 mL) butter 3 Tbsp (45 mL) honey	Melt the butter and honey in a saucepan. Remove from the heat.
3 Tbsp (45 mL) whipping cream ¾ cup (175 mL) brown sugar 3 egg yolks 1 tsp (5 mL) vanilla extract	Add the cream, sugar, egg yolks and vanilla extract. Whisk until blended.
	Stir in the coconut and macadamia nuts, and pour into the pre-baked tart shell. Bake for 20 minutes, until golden brown and just set.

Makes 8 servings

Lemon Citron Tarte

from The Lazy Gourmet

Deborah Roitberg shared this recipe with me when she returned from a trip to France. I am forever grateful. My sister Lynn makes it regularly for her catering customers in Toronto. It's always a hit!

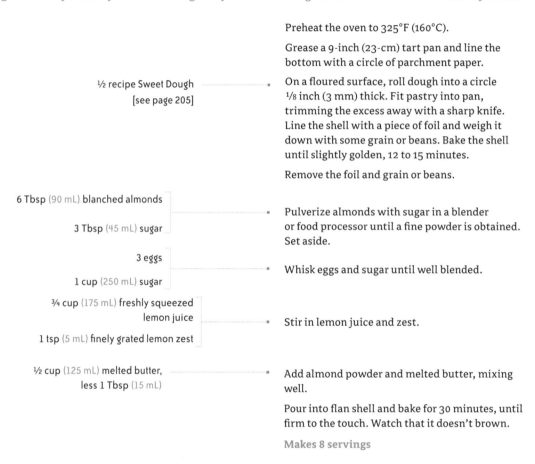

Preheat the oven to 325°F (160°C).

Grease a 9-inch (23-cm) tart pan and line the bottom with a circle of parchment paper.

½ recipe Sweet Dough [see page 205]

On a floured surface, roll dough into a circle ⅛ inch (3 mm) thick. Fit pastry into pan, trimming the excess away with a sharp knife. Line the shell with a piece of foil and weigh it down with some grain or beans. Bake the shell until slightly golden, 12 to 15 minutes.

Remove the foil and grain or beans.

6 Tbsp (90 mL) blanched almonds

3 Tbsp (45 mL) sugar

Pulverize almonds with sugar in a blender or food processor until a fine powder is obtained. Set aside.

3 eggs

1 cup (250 mL) sugar

Whisk eggs and sugar until well blended.

¾ cup (175 mL) freshly squeezed lemon juice

1 tsp (5 mL) finely grated lemon zest

Stir in lemon juice and zest.

½ cup (125 mL) melted butter, less 1 Tbsp (15 mL)

Add almond powder and melted butter, mixing well.

Pour into flan shell and bake for 30 minutes, until firm to the touch. Watch that it doesn't brown.

Makes 8 servings

Lemon Tarts

There's nothing like a sweet homemade tart shell filled with tangy lemon curd and topped with fresh berries. These tarts incorporate my favorite sweet dough. The recipe for the dough was given to The Lazy Gourmet by former pastry chef Lisa Wagner, to whom we are forever grateful. The lemon curd portion of the recipe is from *Fresh Tarts*, which I co-wrote with Deborah Roitberg.

Preheat oven to 350°F (180°C).

½ recipe Sweet Dough
[recipe follows]

Press into small tart shells. Prick each shell with a fork. Bake in preheated oven for 10 to 12 minutes until golden. Let cool.

Luscious Lemon Curd

1¼ cups (300 mL) sugar

¾ cup (175 mL) fresh lemon juice

4 whole eggs

4 egg yolks

Whisk all ingredients together in top of double boiler over simmering water until mixture thickens enough to coat the back of a spoon. Remove top portion of double boiler and place on countertop.

14 Tbsp (200 mL) unsalted butter, softened

Gradually whisk in butter, 1 Tbsp (15 mL) at a time, until incorporated.

Transfer to a glass bowl. Cool to room temperature. Refrigerate up to 2 weeks.

When cooled, drop by spoonfuls into the tarts.

Makes enough for 4 dozen small tarts

tip: The full recipe of Sweet Dough will make more tart shells than you will have filling for. Pre-baked tart shells can be frozen for future use.

Sweet Dough

2 cups (500 mL) all-purpose flour

⅓ cup (75 mL) sugar

Combine flour and sugar.

1 cup (250 mL) butter, softened

With a pastry cutter, blend in butter until it forms coarse crumbs.

2 egg yolks

Add yolks one at a time, mixing only until the dough comes away from the sides of the bowl.

Roll into 2 balls. Flatten and wrap in plastic wrap. Chill until needed.

Makes two 9-inch (23-cm) tart shells

White Chocolate Mousse Bombe

from *The Lazy Gourmet*

Your guests will never believe how easy it was to make this confection. And fun, too! My daughter Mira has been playing with the plastique since she was very little.

Preheat the oven to 350°F (180°C).

Line the bottom of a 9-inch (2.5-L) springform pan with a circle of parchment paper.

Base

4 oz (125 g) semi-sweet chocolate — Melt chocolate in a double boiler or microwave and let cool.

½ cup (125 mL) butter
1 cup (250 mL) sugar — Cream butter with sugar.

2 egg yolks — Slowly blend in egg yolks.

3 Tbsp (45 mL) hot water — Add melted chocolate to sugar mixture, then add hot water and mix well.

½ cup (125 mL) all-purpose flour — Add the flour and mix until just blended.

2 egg whites — Beat the egg whites until soft peaks form. Fold into chocolate mixture. Pour into the springform pan.

Bake in preheated oven for 20 minutes. Do not overbake. Cool on a rack.

Chocolate Plastique Topping

6 oz (175 g) semi-sweet chocolate
4 Tbsp (60 mL) corn syrup — For the topping, melt chocolate in a double boiler. Add corn syrup and mix until well blended.

Form the mixture into a ball. Place it between 2 sheets of waxed paper and roll with a rolling pin until it is 16 inches (38 cm) in diameter. Leaving it between the sheets of waxed paper, place it in the refrigerator. It will remain pliable when cooled.

>>

White Chocolate Mousse

1⅔ cup (400 mL) whipping cream ⸺⸺⸺⸺ Heat cream until it's steaming.

9 oz (300 g) finely chopped white chocolate ⸺⸺⸺ Pour over white chocolate and whisk until blended.

Chill for 3 hours, or, for better results, overnight in the fridge. Whip with electric mixer until thickened. Scoop white chocolate mousse over base and mold it into a dome shape. Place it back in the fridge until well set, from 2 to 3 hours.

Carefully remove domed cake from pan and set on a serving platter. Remove chocolate plastique from the fridge and centre it on top of domed cake. Gently press chocolate around cake and cut off the excess at the base.

Save the excess pieces and make decorations such as stars, roses or letters to decorate the top of the bombe.

Makes 8 to 10 servings

No-Fail Pastry

from *The Expo 86 Cookbook*

Another recipe given to me by my friend Roberta Niemann. Still and always a favorite!

2½ cups (625 mL) all-purpose flour

½ tsp (5 mL) salt

½ cup (125 mL) butter

½ cup (125 mL) shortening

Stir salt into flour. Cut butter and shortening into flour.

1 egg yolk

juice of ½ lemon

water

Combine egg yolk and lemon juice and add water to make ½ cup (125 mL) of liquid. Add to flour mixture. Mix until just blended.

Roll into a ball and refrigerate until ready to use.

Makes double crust for one 9-inch (23-cm) or 10-inch (25-cm) pie

Grandma Faye's Blueberry Pie

My mouth waters when I even think about this pie! It *must* be made during blueberry season every summer.

Preheat oven to 425°F (220°C).

⅓ cup (75 mL) flour

1 cup (250 mL) sugar

1 tsp (5 mL) cinnamon

1 tsp (5 mL) nutmeg

Mix together.

4 cups (1 L) blueberries

1 Tbsp (15 mL) lemon juice

Sprinkle blueberries with lemon juice, then combine with flour mixture.

Pour into pie shell and dot with butter.

one 9- or 10-inch (23- or 25-cm) double pie crust [see No-Fail Pastry, above]

Cover with top crust.

Bake in preheated oven for 15 minutes, then reduce heat to 350°F (180°C) and bake for another 30 minutes.

tip: Be sure to make small slashes in the top crust for the juice to escape. I remember Grandma put-ting macaroni in the creases to act as a stove pipe for the juices.

Makes 8 servings

Poppy Seed Chiffon Cake

This cake is light and crunchy as well because of the poppy seeds.

¾ cup (175 mL) poppy seeds
1 cup (250 mL) warm water

Soak seeds in water for several hours. Do not drain.

Preheat oven to 350°F (180°C).

Grease and flour a 10-inch (4-L) tube pan.

7 egg yolks
2 tsp (10 mL) vanilla extract
½ cup (125 mL) oil
½ tsp (2 mL) baking soda

Add egg yolks, vanilla extract, oil and baking soda to poppy seed liquid and mix well.

2 cups (500 mL) flour
1 Tbsp (15 mL) baking powder
¾ cup (175 mL) white sugar
1 tsp (5 mL) salt

Sift 3 times. Set aside.

7 egg whites
¾ cup (175 mL) white sugar

Beat until stiff.

½ tsp (1 mL) cream of tartar

Add cream of tartar to egg white mixture.

Make a well in flour mixture and add poppy seed mixture. Beat until well blended. Then fold batter into stiffened egg white gradually.

Pour into prepared pan. Bake in preheated oven for 45 minutes to 1 hour. Turn upside down to cool on rack.

When cool, top with Incredible Chocolate Icing (page 199) and/or Cream Cheese Icing (page 192).

Makes 10 to 12 servings

tip: I make this a yin-yang cake by icing half with cream cheese icing and half with chocolate icing.

Almond Fudge Torte

This recipe is so easy to make and is always a hit. I make it with ¼ cup (50 mL) of rice flour in place of all-purpose flour for Uncle Peter, who suffers from celiac disease, and it's equally delicious!

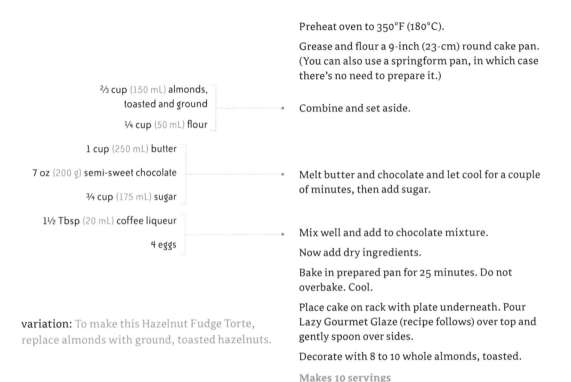

Preheat oven to 350°F (180°C).

Grease and flour a 9-inch (23-cm) round cake pan. (You can also use a springform pan, in which case there's no need to prepare it.)

⅔ cup (150 mL) almonds, toasted and ground
¼ cup (50 mL) flour

Combine and set aside.

1 cup (250 mL) butter
7 oz (200 g) semi-sweet chocolate
¾ cup (175 mL) sugar

Melt butter and chocolate and let cool for a couple of minutes, then add sugar.

1½ Tbsp (20 mL) coffee liqueur
4 eggs

Mix well and add to chocolate mixture.

Now add dry ingredients.

Bake in prepared pan for 25 minutes. Do not overbake. Cool.

Place cake on rack with plate underneath. Pour Lazy Gourmet Glaze (recipe follows) over top and gently spoon over sides.

Decorate with 8 to 10 whole almonds, toasted.

Makes 10 servings

variation: To make this Hazelnut Fudge Torte, replace almonds with ground, toasted hazelnuts.

Lazy Gourmet Glaze

A variation of this recipe appeared in *Nuts about Chocolate*, a book I wrote with former partner Deborah Roitberg. It was then republished in *Chocolatier* magazine.

¼ cup (50 mL) butter
4 oz (125 g) semi-sweet chocolate

Melt together.

2 Tbsp (30 mL) whipping cream
1 Tbsp (15 mL) coffee liqueur

Mix and blend into above.

Makes about ½ cup (125 mL)

Lemon Alaska Torte

from *Mama Never Cooked Like This*

This book wouldn't be complete without this wonderful, easy recipe! If you wish, use store-bought ladyfingers. That's what Roz, the "Mama" from *Mama Never Cooked Like This,* does!

Preheat the oven to 350°F (180°C).

Line a baking sheet with parchment paper.

Ladyfingers

½ cup (125 mL) sifted flour

⅔ cup (150 mL) icing sugar

Sift together flour and half the sugar. Set aside.

3 egg whites

½ tsp (2 mL) vanilla extract

Beat egg whites until stiff. Continue beating, and gradually add rest of sugar and vanilla extract.

3 egg yolks

In a separate bowl beat egg yolks until stiff. Then fold into egg white mixture.

Sift the flour mixture again over egg mixture and gently fold together.

Press the batter through a pastry bag to form three ½-inch (1-cm) strips on prepared baking sheet. Bake in preheated oven for 12 to 15 minutes until golden.

Cut ladyfingers to fit 1 inch above top of springform pan, placing side by side around edge of pan.

Makes approximately 24 ladyfingers

Lemon Filling

5 egg yolks

2 egg whites

Combine yolks and whites in top of double boiler.

¾ cup (175 mL) fresh lemon juice [about 6 lemons]

grated rind of 1 lemon

1¼ cups (300 mL) sugar

Add lemon juice, rind and sugar to above and beat. Cook over boiling water stirring constantly until thick. Then remove from heat and cool.

2 cups (500 mL) whipping cream

Whip cream until soft peaks form. Fold into above mixture.

Line sides and base of 9-inch (2.5-L) springform pan with ladyfingers. Pour in filling and freeze.

Meringue

3 egg whites

Beat egg whites until stiff.

4 Tbsp (60 mL) sugar

Gradually add sugar.

Cover torte with meringue. Place briefly under broiler until brown. Freeze again before serving!

Makes 8 to 10 servings

Your Basic Chocolate Cheesecake

For many years people begged me for this recipe. The original was a Saskatoon recipe given to me by Miriam Gropper, but she insists that the credit go to Arlene Gladstone.

Preheat oven to 350°F (180°C).

Chocolate Crust

1½ cups (325 mL) chocolate wafers, crushed

⅓ cup (75 mL) butter, melted

Mix and press into a 9- or 10-inch (23- or 25-cm) springform pan. Bake for 5 minutes.

Filling

1 lb (500 g) spreadable cream cheese

⅔ cup (150 mL) sour cream

½ cup (125 mL) sugar

2 tsp (10 mL) vanilla extract

Combine and beat until smooth.

7 oz (200 g) semi-sweet chocolate

1 oz (25 g) bitter chocolate

Melt over hot water and add to mixture, beating until smooth.

2 large eggs

Add and beat for 5 minutes.

Pour filling into crust. Bake in preheated oven 40 to 45 minutes.

options:

Whipped Cream Topping

1 cup (250 mL) whipping cream

3 Tbsp (45 mL) icing sugar

1 tsp (5 mL) vanilla extract

Beat until soft peaks form. Spread over chilled cheesecake.

Sour Cream Topping

1 cup (250 mL) sour cream

1–2 Tbsp (15–30 mL) your favorite flavouring

2 Tbsp (30 mL) sugar

Mix and spoon gently over cheesecake and return to oven for 5 minutes.

Garnish (for either topping)

2 oz (50 g) shaved chocolate or nuts

Sprinkle with shaved chocolate and/or nuts. Chill 2 to 3 hours before serving.

Makes 10 to 12 servings

>>

variations:

for Chocolate Brandy Cheesecake
Omit vanilla extract and add in its place:
1 Tbsp (15 mL) brandy

for Chocolate Orange Cheesecake
Add to batter with vanilla extract:
1 Tbsp (15 mL) orange juice concentrate
1 Tbsp (15 mL) orange liqueur

for Chocolate Amaretto Cheesecake
Add to batter with vanilla extract:
1 Tbsp (15 mL) almond liqueur
1 Tbsp (15 mL) almond extract

Lynn's Chocolate Pudding Cake

People have been begging Lynn for this recipe. She has finally agreed to share it.

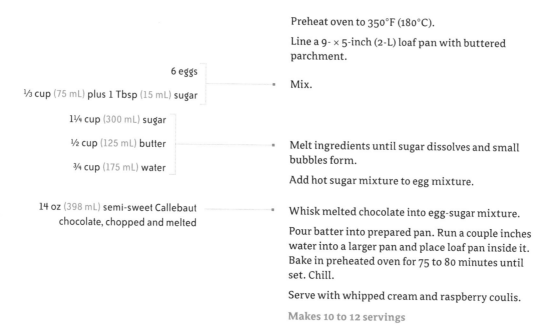

Preheat oven to 350°F (180°C).

Line a 9- × 5-inch (2-L) loaf pan with buttered parchment.

6 eggs
⅓ cup (75 mL) plus 1 Tbsp (15 mL) sugar

Mix.

1¼ cup (300 mL) sugar
½ cup (125 mL) butter
¾ cup (175 mL) water

Melt ingredients until sugar dissolves and small bubbles form.

Add hot sugar mixture to egg mixture.

14 oz (398 mL) semi-sweet Callebaut chocolate, chopped and melted

Whisk melted chocolate into egg-sugar mixture.

Pour batter into prepared pan. Run a couple inches water into a larger pan and place loaf pan inside it. Bake in preheated oven for 75 to 80 minutes until set. Chill.

Serve with whipped cream and raspberry coulis.

Makes 10 to 12 servings

Chocolate Caramel Turtle Flan

There's something magical about homemade caramel. Many recipes suggest melting store-bought caramels, but the taste and texture just aren't there.

Preheat the oven to 325°F (160°C).

Grease a 9-inch (23-cm) tart pan and line the bottom with a circle of parchment paper.

6 oz (175 g) semi-sweet chocolate, broken into pieces

¼ cup (50 mL) sugar

4 Tbsp (60 mL) unsalted butter, sizzling hot

Cuisinart-process chocolate, sugar and hot butter until fine. Pour hot chocolate through tube.

2 large eggs

2 Tbsp (30 mL) flour

Add eggs and flour to hot chocolate.

1 recipe Sweet Dough [see page 205]

On a floured surface, roll dough into a circle ⅛ inch (3 mm) thick. Fit pastry into prepared pan, trimming the excess away with a sharp knife. Line the shell with a piece of foil and weigh it down with some grain or beans. Bake the shell until slightly golden, 12 to 15 minutes.

Remove the foil and grain or beans. Increase oven heat to 350°F (180°).

Pour chocolate filling into pre-baked shell and bake about 17 minutes until set around edges but slightly soft in centre.

Caramel Topping

½ cup (125 mL) whipping cream

4 Tbsp (60 mL) unsalted butter

Bring cream and butter to simmer in a small saucepan.

1 cup (250 mL) sugar

In a separate saucepan heat sugar until it melts.

2 Tbsp (30 mL) corn syrup

Add corn syrup and boil until tan-coloured, about 6 minutes.

Remove from heat and add hot cream mixture. Return to high heat and cook until smooth and thickened (about 2 minutes).

1 tsp (5 mL) vanilla extract

Add vanilla extract.

Pour warm caramel over tart.

½ cup (125 mL) chopped pecans, toasted

Sprinkle around edge of tart.

tip: Serve at room temperature, not cold!

Makes 8 servings

Homemade Marshmallows

People have been begging me for this recipe. It's sticky to deal with, but the results are magnificent. You'll never buy another packaged marshmallow.

Line cookie sheet with parchment paper.

1 oz (25 g) gelatin powder
2 cups (500 mL) white corn syrup
2 cups (500 mL) white sugar
¾ cup (175 mL) water

Mix together in a medium saucepan, and cook until the temperature reaches 240°F (116°C).

4 egg whites

Beat until soft peaks form. Slowly add the hot syrup in a steady stream. Beat until glossy, 8 to 10 minutes. Pour onto lined cookie sheet, then leave overnight.

To serve, cut with a hot knife into small squares.

Makes 8 dozen marshmallows

variations:
Toasted coconut: lightly sprinkle with water and roll in toasted coconut.
Milk or dark chocolate: Dip the marshmallow pieces into melted chocolate.

Skor Bar Cake

Thank you to Deborah Roitberg for the best cake ever! The caramel glaze is for those with sweet teeth.

Preheat the oven to 350°F (175°C).

Lightly spray with cooking oil a 10-inch (4.5-L) tube pan.

3 cups (750 mL) flour
1 tsp (5 mL) salt
2 tsp (10 mL) baking powder

Sift and set aside.

7 Skor chocolate bars

Chop coarsely, sprinkle with 1 Tbsp (15 mL) flour and set aside.

1 cup (250 mL) butter, softened
3 Tbsp (45 mL) vegetable shortening

Using an electric beater, in a large bowl, cream butter and shortening well.

1⅞ cup (475 mL) berry sugar

Add very slowly.

4 eggs

Add eggs, one at a time, beating well after each addition.

1 Tbsp (15 mL) vanilla extract

Add and beat for 5 minutes (yes!).

1 cup (250 mL) milk

Gently mix in one-third of flour mixture; then half of milk; one-third of flour mixture; last of milk; last of flour mixture.

Gently fold in the Skor pieces.

Pour into prepared pan.

Bake in preheated oven for 55 to 60 minutes until it tests done. (A clean toothpick tells the story!)

Invert and remove from pan. Cool completely before topping with Caramel Glaze (recipe follows).

Makes 10 to 12 servings

Caramel Glaze

½ cup (125 mL) butter
1 cup (250 mL) brown sugar

Heat until melted. With paper towel, clean the sides of the pan.

Increase heat to high and bring to boil. At boiling point, reduce to medium. Boil 1 minute. Remove from heat.

¼ cup (50 mL) milk

Add milk and stir until blended. Whisk 1 minute.

2 cups (500 mL) [approximately] sifted icing sugar

Add 1 cup (250 mL) icing sugar to mixture and whisk until smooth. Continue adding more icing sugar gradually, until the glaze coats a spoon. Whisk again and pour over cake.

Makes 2 cups (500 mL)

Easy Homemade Vanilla Ice Cream

I developed this recipe at the lake and make it every summer to eat with fresh summer berries and other fruit. It's also delicious served with Lynn's Hot Fudge Sauce (page 96).

4 cups (1 L) half-and-half
1 vanilla bean, split

In medium saucepan, heat on medium heat until hot. Remove vanilla bean.

6 egg yolks
1 cup (250 mL) sugar

Whisk together.

Then add 2 cups (500 mL) of hot cream to yolk mixture.

Pour this mixture back into the pot with the remaining cream.

Reduce to medium-low heat and stir until mixture thickens (7 to 9 minutes). Do not let mixture boil!

Strain mixture into bowl. Whisk an additional 1 minute.

Cool on countertop.

1 Tbsp (15 mL) vanilla extract

Add vanilla.

Chill at least 3 to 4 hours.

Transfer to ice cream machine and follow manufacturer's instructions.

Makes 8 servings

CHAPTER NINE

Squares and Cookies

Tout Sweet Cappuccino Truffles

Thanks to Anna DeFlores from Tout Sweet for sharing this recipe with Deborah Roitberg and me in the early eighties. It's still a classic today!

8 oz (250 g) semi-sweet chocolate ¼ cup (50 mL) butter	Melt and remove from heat. Beat together until blended.
2 tsp (10 mL) instant coffee	Add.
¼ cup (50 mL) evaporated milk	Add.
	Chill until set. Roll into balls. Freeze for 1 hour.
4 oz (125 g) white chocolate, melted	Dip frozen truffles into white chocolate. Remove quickly to prevent dark chocolate from melting into white.
	Chill until ready to serve.

Makes about 20 truffles

Lazy Gourmet Shortbread

You will never need another shortbread cookie recipe! We have been making this shortbread recipe at Christmastime at The Lazy Gourmet for the past 27 Christmases. Customers have asked for it for just as long, but this is the first time it's been published.

1 cup (250 mL) butter ½ cup (125 mL) icing sugar 2 cups (500 mL) flour ½ tsp (2 mL) salt	Combine all ingredients. Chill for 1 hour.
	Preheat the oven to 350°F (180°C).
	Line 2 baking sheets with parchment paper.
	Roll dough out onto floured board, and cut into rectangles or use cookie cutters to make your favorite shapes.
	Bake in preheated oven for 10 minutes until golden brown.

Makes 36 cookies

Dream Bars

from *Mama Never Cooked Like This*

This is a recipe that I developed as a teenager and still love today. Leave out the chocolate and you have a butterscotch bar.

Preheat oven to 350°F (180°C).

Grease an 8-inch (2-L) square baking pan.

½ cup (125 mL) butter
1 cup (250 mL) flour
½ cup (125 mL) brown sugar

Mix together and pat down in prepared pan.

Bake in preheated oven for 10 minutes.

Reduce heat to 325°F (160°C).

2 eggs
1 cup (250 mL) brown sugar
3 Tbsp (45 mL) flour
1 tsp (5 mL) vanilla extract
½ tsp (2 mL) salt
1 cup (250 mL) chocolate chips
1 cup (250 mL) chopped walnuts

Mix together and pour over crust.

Bake for another 20 minutes.

Makes 16 bars

Coconut Meringues

from *Mama Never Cooked Like This*

This is another favorite recipe from Grandma Faye!

Preheat oven to 250°F (120°C).

Line a baking sheet with parchment paper.

3 egg whites — Beat until stiff, then continue beating for 3 minutes.

⅔ cup (150 mL) granulated sugar — Slowly add sugar, continuing to beat until egg whites are stiff and glossy.

1½ cups (360 mL) long-thread coconut
1 cup (250 mL) chopped walnuts — Mix together and fold into above.

1 tsp (5 mL) vanilla extract — Add at end.

Drop by spoonfuls onto prepared baking sheet.

Bake in preheated oven for 45 minutes.

Makes 30 meringues

Amaretti

This is a great recipe for people with wheat allergies. Also is a great Passover recipe. Very versatile!

Preheat oven to 350°F (180°C).

Spray a baking sheet with cooking oil.

1 cup (250 mL) almond meal [ground almonds]
1 cup (250 mL) sugar
2 egg whites — Beat with electric mixer for 3 minutes. Let stand for 5 minutes.

Spoon mixture gently into piping bag with ½-inch (1-cm) plain tube. Pipe onto prepared baking sheet in a circular motion from centre out. Place cookies 2 inches (5 cm) apart.

24 blanched almonds — Place an almond on top of each cookie.

Bake in preheated oven for about 12 minutes until light brown.

Makes 24 cookies

Coconut Caramel Squares

from *Mama Never Cooked Like This*

My earliest childhood food memory. Probably why I have such a sweet tooth!

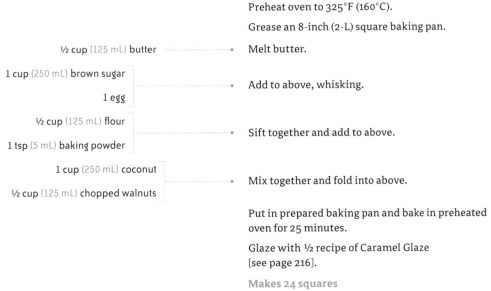

½ cup (125 mL) butter — Preheat oven to 325°F (160°C).

Grease an 8-inch (2-L) square baking pan.

½ cup (125 mL) butter — Melt butter.

1 cup (250 mL) brown sugar
1 egg — Add to above, whisking.

½ cup (125 mL) flour
1 tsp (5 mL) baking powder — Sift together and add to above.

1 cup (250 mL) coconut
½ cup (125 mL) chopped walnuts — Mix together and fold into above.

Put in prepared baking pan and bake in preheated oven for 25 minutes.

Glaze with ½ recipe of Caramel Glaze [see page 216].

Makes 24 squares

tip: This recipe was adapted from the Coconut Ginger Squares in *Mama* …. I omitted the candied ginger here because kids often find ginger too strong-tasting. Feel free to put it back in yourself (¼ cup (50 mL) candied ginger, chopped).

Toasted Almond Buttercrunch

from *Mama Never Cooked Like This*

People tell me that they've been making this buttercrunch for Christmas presents for 25 years!

Preheat the oven to 350°F (180°C).

Grease a 9-inch (2.5-L) square baking pan.

1 cup (250 mL) almonds

Toast almonds in preheated oven for 10 minutes, then spread in bottom of prepared baking pan.

1 cup (250 mL) butter

1 cup (250 mL) sugar

Cook on medium heat until candy thermometer reaches 310°F (155°C). Important: do not stir.

Remove from heat and pour over toasted almonds. Cool until hardened.

3–4 oz (75–125 g) semi-sweet chocolate

Melt chocolate over hot water. Do not allow water to boil.

Spread over above.

⅓ cup (75 mL) walnuts, crushed

Sprinkle crushed walnuts over chocolate while warm.

Makes 2 lb (1 kg)

Toffee Bars

from *Let Me in the Kitchen*

My sister Lynn still uses this recipe for her catering. She cuts them into delicate bars. I eat the edges!

Preheat the oven to 350°F (180°C).

Grease a 12- × 16-inch (2.5-L) baking sheet.

1 cup (250 mL) soft butter — Cream butter.

1 cup (250 mL) brown sugar — Add brown sugar and mix until blended.

2 cups (500 mL) flour, white or whole wheat — Add flour and stir until the mixture is almost blended. Then use your hands to make the mixture smooth.

1 cup (250 mL) pure chocolate chips or carob chips

½ cup (125 mL) walnut or pecan pieces — Stir in the chips, nuts and vanilla extract.

1 tsp (5 mL) vanilla extract

Spread mixture onto prepared baking sheet.

Bake for 25 minutes until golden brown. Remove from oven and cut into bars while still warm. (If the toffee cools before you cut it, it will crack.)

Makes 48 bars

Heavenly Chocolate Chip Cookies

from *Let Me in the Kitchen*

For those who prefer a lighter and crisper chocolate chip cookie. Kids still love this recipe and I get calls about how easy it is for them.

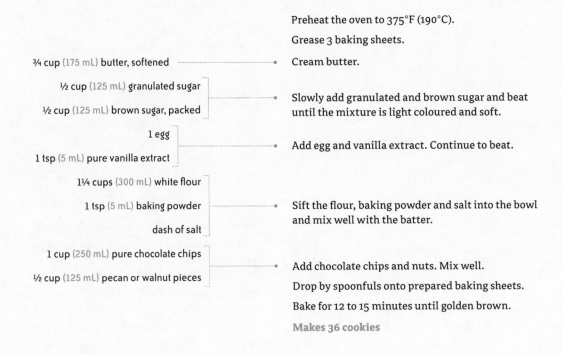

Preheat the oven to 375°F (190°C).

Grease 3 baking sheets.

¾ cup (175 mL) butter, softened —— Cream butter.

½ cup (125 mL) granulated sugar
½ cup (125 mL) brown sugar, packed

Slowly add granulated and brown sugar and beat until the mixture is light coloured and soft.

1 egg
1 tsp (5 mL) pure vanilla extract

Add egg and vanilla extract. Continue to beat.

1¼ cups (300 mL) white flour
1 tsp (5 mL) baking powder
dash of salt

Sift the flour, baking powder and salt into the bowl and mix well with the batter.

1 cup (250 mL) pure chocolate chips
½ cup (125 mL) pecan or walnut pieces

Add chocolate chips and nuts. Mix well.

Drop by spoonfuls onto prepared baking sheets.

Bake for 12 to 15 minutes until golden brown.

Makes 36 cookies

Blondies

from *Let Me in the Kitchen*

When the Lazy Gourmet was on Fourth Avenue, people used to wait for these Blondies to come out of the oven.

Preheat the oven to 350°F (180°C).

Lightly grease a 9- × 13-inch (3.5-L) square baking pan.

1 cup (250 mL) butter — Melt butter in a small pot over low heat.

2 cups (500 mL) brown sugar — Put sugar into a large bowl and pour butter over it. Mix well with a whisk.

4 eggs — Break eggs into a small bowl. Mix with a whisk until the whites and yolks are blended.

Add to the butter-sugar mixture.

1½ cups (375 mL) white flour
2 tsp (10 mL) baking powder

Sift flour and baking powder into the mixture. Mix with a whisk.

2 cups (500 mL) pure chocolate or carob chips
1½ cups (375 mL) walnut pieces

Add ¾ cup (200 mL) each of chips and nuts.

2 tsp (10 mL) pure vanilla extract — Add vanilla extract and mix with the wooden spoon.

Pour mixture into prepared pan. Sprinkle remaining chips and nuts over top. Bake for 30 minutes.

Cut the Blondies into squares and enjoy!

Makes 20 squares

Homemade Chocolate Mints

This recipe was borrowed from *Nuts about Chocolate* and slightly altered. It's a melt-in-your-mouth explosion of rich chocolate and mint flavour.

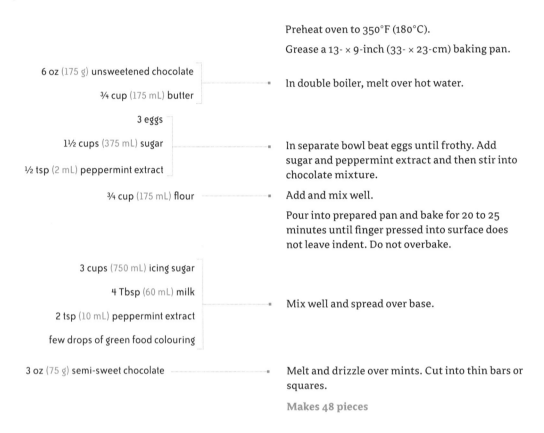

Preheat oven to 350°F (180°C).

Grease a 13- × 9-inch (33- × 23-cm) baking pan.

6 oz (175 g) unsweetened chocolate
¾ cup (175 mL) butter

In double boiler, melt over hot water.

3 eggs
1½ cups (375 mL) sugar
½ tsp (2 mL) peppermint extract

In separate bowl beat eggs until frothy. Add sugar and peppermint extract and then stir into chocolate mixture.

¾ cup (175 mL) flour

Add and mix well.

Pour into prepared pan and bake for 20 to 25 minutes until finger pressed into surface does not leave indent. Do not overbake.

3 cups (750 mL) icing sugar
4 Tbsp (60 mL) milk
2 tsp (10 mL) peppermint extract
few drops of green food colouring

Mix well and spread over base.

3 oz (75 g) semi-sweet chocolate

Melt and drizzle over mints. Cut into thin bars or squares.

Makes 48 pieces

L.G. Bars

from *The Expo 86 Cookbook*

L.G. stands for Lazy Gourmet, where this confection was invented. If you are shy of sweets, stay away!

Grease a 9-inch (2.5-L) square baking pan.

Layer One

½ cup (125 mL) butter, softened

¼ cup (50 mL) sugar

1 egg

1 tsp (5 mL) vanilla extract

Mix together, then set over boiling water. Stir until slightly thickened.

2 cups (500 mL) vanilla wafer crumbs or graham wafer crumbs

1 cup (250mL) desiccated coconut

½ cup (125 mL) chopped hazelnuts, toasted

Combine and add to above.

Press mixture into prepared pan, pressing down to spread evenly. Let stand 15 minutes.

Layer Two

¼ cup (50 mL) butter, softened

2 Tbsp (30 mL) milk

2½ cups (625 mL) icing sugar

2 tsp (10 mL) instant coffee, dissolved in 2 Tbsp (30 mL) hot coffee

¼ cup (50 mL) cocoa powder

Mix well and spread over Layer One. Refrigerate 15 minutes.

Layer Three

6 oz (175 g) white chocolate

Melt over hot (not boiling) water, then gently spread over Layer Two.

Chill until just set. Cut into squares and go crazy!

Makes 20 bars

Lazy Gourmet Mocha Nanaimo Bars

from *The Expo 86 Cookbook*

Nanaimo Bars were first sold commercially at The Lazy Gourmet. Now, they can be purchased all across Canada.

Grease a 9-inch (2.5-L) square baking pan.

Layer One

½ cup (125 mL) butter
¼ cup (50 mL) sugar
1 egg
1 tsp (10 mL) vanilla extract
2 Tbsp (30 mL) cocoa powder

Mix together and set over boiling water. Stir until slightly thickened.

2 cups (500 mL) graham wafer crumbs
1 cup (250 mL) long-thread coconut
½ cup (125 mL) chopped walnuts or pecans

Add to above.

Press mixture into prepared pan, pressing down to spread evenly. Let stand 15 minutes.

Layer Two

¼ cup (50 mL) butter, softened
2 Tbsp (30 mL) milk
2 cups (500 mL) icing sugar
2 tsp (10 mL) instant coffee, dissolved in 2 Tbsp (30 mL) hot coffee
2 Tbsp (30 mL) custard powder
1 tsp (5 mL) coffee liqueur [optional]

Mix well together and spread over Layer One.

Layer Three

5 oz (150 g) semi-sweet chocolate

Melt chocolate over hot (not boiling) water.

1 Tbsp (15 mL) butter

Very slowly stir in butter. Spread over Layer Two. Refrigerate, then cut into squares.

Makes 20 bars

>>

variations:

Traditional Nanaimo Bars

Substitute for Layer Two

¼ cup (50 mL) butter, softened

3 Tbsp (45 mL) milk

2 cups (500 mL) icing sugar

2 Tbsp (30 mL) custard powder

Mix together and spread over Layer One.

Mint Nanaimo Bars

Substitute for Layer Two

¼ cup (50 mL) butter, softened

3 Tbsp (45 mL) milk

2 cups (500 mL) icing sugar

2 Tbsp (30 mL) custard powder

½ tsp (2 mL) mint extract

few drops of red or green food colouring

Mix together and spread over Layer One.

Money-Back Guarantee Brownies

from Mama Never wwCooked Like This

Preheat oven to 350°F (180°C).

Grease and flour a 13- × 9-inch (33- × 23-cm) baking pan.

1 cup (250 mL) butter · · · · · · · · · · ▪ Melt butter.

1 cup (250 mL) granulated sugar

1 cup (250 mL) brown sugar · · · · · · ▪ Add and blend well.

¾ cup (175 mL) cocoa powder

3 large eggs · · · · · · · · · · · · · · · ▪ Beat in, one at a time.

1 cup (250 mL) flour

· · · · · · ▪ Sift into mixture and stir.

1½ tsp (7 mL) baking powder

1½ tsp (7 mL) vanilla extract

· · · · · · ▪ Add and combine well.

1 cup (250 mL) walnuts, chopped

Pour into prepared pan and bake in preheated oven for 25 to 30 minutes. Do not overbake—centre should be firm but not hard. Allow to cool.

Ice with ½ recipe of Incredible Chocolate Icing (see page 199).

Makes 36 brownies

Peanut Butter Brownies

from Food to Grow On

These are a terrific brownie with the benefit of peanut butter to add some protein. Not a snack to eat every day, but good for the occasional treat!

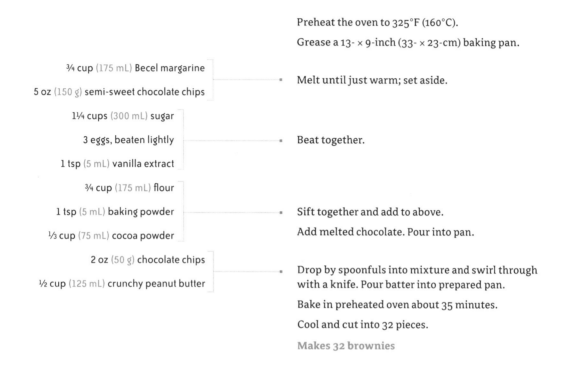

Preheat the oven to 325°F (160°C).

Grease a 13- × 9-inch (33- × 23-cm) baking pan.

¾ cup (175 mL) Becel margarine
5 oz (150 g) semi-sweet chocolate chips

Melt until just warm; set aside.

1¼ cups (300 mL) sugar
3 eggs, beaten lightly
1 tsp (5 mL) vanilla extract

Beat together.

¾ cup (175 mL) flour
1 tsp (5 mL) baking powder
⅓ cup (75 mL) cocoa powder

Sift together and add to above.

Add melted chocolate. Pour into pan.

2 oz (50 g) chocolate chips
½ cup (125 mL) crunchy peanut butter

Drop by spoonfuls into mixture and swirl through with a knife. Pour batter into prepared pan.

Bake in preheated oven about 35 minutes.

Cool and cut into 32 pieces.

Makes 32 brownies

Black and White Brownies

from *The Lazy Gourmet*

This is a combination cheesecake and square rolled into one. The squares are firmer and cut more easily than cheesecake.

Preheat the oven to 325°F (165°C).

Lightly grease a 13- × 9-inch (33- × 23-cm) baking pan.

Base

6 oz (175 g) semi-sweet chocolate — Melt chocolate in the top of a double boiler. Remove from heat and let cool to lukewarm.

¾ cup (175 mL) butter
1 cup (250 mL) sugar — Beat butter and sugar together.

3 eggs — Add eggs, 1 at a time.

¾ cup (175 mL) all-purpose flour — Fold in flour.

Reserve 1 cup (250 mL) of the batter and spread the remainder into the prepared pan.

Mix chocolate into reserved batter, but do not overbeat.

Cream Cheese Topping

1 lb (500 g) spreadable cream cheese
⅔ cup (150 mL) sugar — Mix cream cheese and sugar together.

4 eggs — Add eggs one at a time, beating well with each addition.

Spead cream cheese topping over the base. Drop reserved chocolate batter over the cream cheese topping and swirl to create a marble effect.

Bake 40 to 45 minutes until set.

Refrigerate before serving.

Makes 24 brownies

Rocky Roads

from *The Lazy Gourmet*

When I bought the lease to Bridges Bagel Deli, I was really paying to buy this fabulous recipe. It's great as a Passover square as well, because it has no flour!

Preheat the oven to 350°F (180°C).

Lightly grease a 13- × 9-inch (33- × 23-cm) baking pan.

1 cup (250 mL) butter

2 lb (1 kg) semi-sweet chocolate

Melt butter and chocolate in the top of a double boiler. Allow to cool.

1½ cups (360 mL) hazelnuts

2 cups (500 mL) whole almonds

Toast nuts on a cookie sheet in preheated oven for 10 to 12 minutes until golden. Cool.

one 10-oz (285-g) bag mini marshmallows

Stir marshmallows and nuts into the slightly cooled chocolate mixture. Spread into prepared pan. Refrigerate for 2 to 3 hours. Cut into small squares.

Makes 30 squares

Million Dollar Bar or Almond Crunch

from The Lazy Gourmet

Preheat oven to 350°F (180°C).

Line a 17- × 12-inch (2.5-L) jelly roll pan with parchment paper.

1 cup (250 mL) sugar

1 cup (250 mL) brown sugar

1½ cups (360 mL) cold butter, cubed

2 egg yolks

½ tsp (2 mL) vanilla extract

Mix together in order shown.

2 cups (500 mL) flour

pinch of salt

Add to above.

Using heel of hand (or rolling pin), flatten mixture into prepared jelly roll pan. Bake for 45 minutes in centre of oven.

9 oz (300 g) milk chocolate, preferably Belgian or Swiss

Melt chocolate and spread on warm baked dough.

1 cup (250 mL) flaked or slivered almonds, toasted until golden

Sprinkle nuts over top.

Cut into 2-inch (5-cm) squares while still warm.

Makes 40 bars

tip: I started with Belgian Callebaut for this recipe and graduated to Swiss Lindt. Both are great! Often kids don't like nuts, so feel free to omit them if desired.

Lemon Squares

from *The Lazy Gourmet*

People go crazy for these squares! The freshly squeezed lemon juice is what makes them so special. Don't be put off by the amount of sugar in this recipe. Keep in mind how much lemon juice there is to balance it out!

Preheat the oven to 350°F (180°C).

Grease a 13- × 9-inch (33- × 23-cm) baking pan.

Base

1½ cups (360 mL) white flour

6 Tbsp (90 mL) sugar

¾ cup (175 mL) butter

Mix until well blended.

Press into prepared pan. Bake in preheated oven for 18 to 20 minutes until golden brown.

Topping

5 large eggs

2 egg yolks

2½ cups (625 mL) sugar

Beat eggs, yolks and sugar.

1 cup (250 mL) freshly squeezed lemon juice

Stir in lemon juice.

¼ cup (50 mL) flour

Add flour last.

Pour over baked crust. Bake in preheated oven for 40 minutes until set. Cool on rack, then chill at least 2 hours.

Use a thin paring knife to cut into small squares.

Makes 48 squares

Pecan Shortbread Squares

from *Nuts about Chocolate*

Still one of our most popular squares. Deborah Roitberg and I originally published this recipe in *Nuts about Chocolate*. I have doubled the caramel on top to give it a chewier and thicker texture.

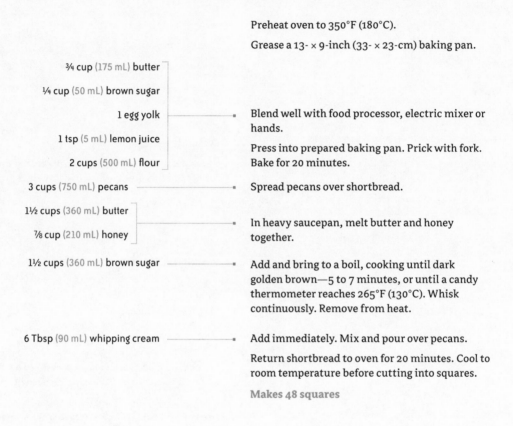

Preheat oven to 350°F (180°C).

Grease a 13- × 9-inch (33- × 23-cm) baking pan.

¾ cup (175 mL) butter

¼ cup (50 mL) brown sugar

1 egg yolk

1 tsp (5 mL) lemon juice

2 cups (500 mL) flour

Blend well with food processor, electric mixer or hands.

Press into prepared baking pan. Prick with fork. Bake for 20 minutes.

3 cups (750 mL) pecans

Spread pecans over shortbread.

1½ cups (360 mL) butter

⅞ cup (210 mL) honey

In heavy saucepan, melt butter and honey together.

1½ cups (360 mL) brown sugar

Add and bring to a boil, cooking until dark golden brown—5 to 7 minutes, or until a candy thermometer reaches 265°F (130°C). Whisk continuously. Remove from heat.

6 Tbsp (90 mL) whipping cream

Add immediately. Mix and pour over pecans.

Return shortbread to oven for 20 minutes. Cool to room temperature before cutting into squares.

Makes 48 squares

Mexican Wedding Shortcakes

This recipe is perfect for a Christmas party tray. The cookies look like snowballs.

Preheat oven to 350°F (150°C).

1 cup (250 mL) butter, softened

½ cup plus 1 Tbsp (140 mL) icing sugar

1 Tbsp (15 mL) vanilla extract

1¾ cups (425 mL) flour

1 cup (250 mL) pecans, finely chopped

Mix together well and drop by teaspoons onto ungreased baking sheet.

½ cup (125 mL) icing sugar

Bake for 25 minutes. When cool, roll in icing sugar.

Makes 4 dozen cookies

tip: These freeze well, but don't roll them in the sugar until thawed.

Lynn's Shortbread Crescents

Truly melt in your mouth. My sister Lynn is an expert at making these shortbread crescents. She makes each crescent as if it's a work of art (which it is!).

Preheat oven to 300°F (150°C).

Line 3 baking sheets with parchment paper.

2½ cups (625 mL) flour

Spread flour on cookie sheets and place under broiler until lightly browned.

1 lb (500 g) butter

1 cup (250 mL) berry sugar

1 cup (250 mL) rice flour

Mix together, then add cooled toasted flour.

2 cups (500 mL) chocolate chunks

Add chocolate chunks to batter and mix well.

Mould into crescents.

Bake in preheated oven for 45 minutes.

8 oz (250 g) chocolate [white, milk, dark or any combination thereof]

When crescents are cool, melt chocolate over hot water. Dip crescents into melted chocolate.

Makes 60 crescents

Cinnamon Almond Shortbread

Grandma Faye always had these great squares on hand. Now my sister Lynn has followed in her footsteps. Store them in an airtight tin to keep them crisp.

Preheat oven to 350°F (180°C).

Grease and flour a 13- × 9-inch (33- × 23-cm) baking pan.

1 cup (250 mL) sugar 1 cup (250 mL) butter	Cream.
1 Tbsp (15 mL) cinnamon 1 tsp (5 mL) vanilla extract 1 cup (250 mL) almonds, ground	Mix and add.
1 egg yolk	Add and mix.
2 cups (500 mL) flour	Add and mix well.

Press onto a prepared baking pan.

1 egg white	Whisk, then spread over shortbread with pastry brush.
1 Tbsp (15 mL) cinnamon 6 Tbsp (90 mL) icing sugar 1 cup (250 mL) almonds, ground	Mix together and sprinkle over shortbread.

Bake for 25 minutes. Cut into squares and separate. Return to warm oven for 25 to 30 minutes to dry out.

Makes 48 squares

Soft Ginger Cookies *with* Oatmeal

from Food to Grow On

Imagine, a delicious ginger cookie with the added nutrition of oats!

Preheat the oven to 350°F (180°C).

Line 2 baking sheets with parchment paper.

2 cups (500 mL) flour

2 tsp (10 mL) ground ginger

¾ tsp (4 mL) ground cinnamon — Sift together.

½ tsp (2 mL) ground cloves

¼ tsp (1 mL) salt

1 cup (250 mL) quick cooking oats — Add to above and set aside.

¾ cup (175 mL) Becel margarine,
or butter, softened — Cream margarine and add sugar gradually.

1 cup (250 mL) sugar

1 egg — Beat into mixture.

1 Tbsp (15 mL) cold water — Stir into above.

¼ cup (50 mL) molasses

Add dry ingredients. Mix until well blended.

2 Tbsp (30 mL) berry sugar — Shape dough into walnut-size balls and roll in berry sugar. Flatten slightly.

Bake in preheated oven for 8 to 10 minutes.

Makes 48 cookies

The Brook Sisters' Flax Spelt Oatmeal Chippers

Paula and Allison Brook graciously shared this recipe with me, even though they knew that I would exploit it to the hilt! These are now the most popular cookies that we sell at The Lazy Gourmet. Our customers were ready for a cookie filled with nutrition.

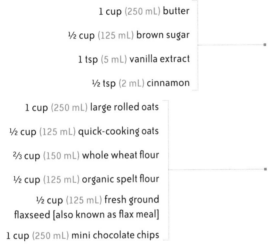

1 cup (250 mL) butter
½ cup (125 mL) brown sugar
1 tsp (5 mL) vanilla extract
½ tsp (2 mL) cinnamon

Cream together until smooth.

1 cup (250 mL) large rolled oats
½ cup (125 mL) quick-cooking oats
⅔ cup (150 mL) whole wheat flour
½ cup (125 mL) organic spelt flour
½ cup (125 mL) fresh ground flaxseed [also known as flax meal]
1 cup (250 mL) mini chocolate chips

One at a time, add these items.

Form into 3 logs; chill 2 hours.

Preheat the oven to 350°F (180°C).

Line 2 baking sheets with parchment paper.

Cut into slices ½ inch (1 cm) thick. Place slices on sheets and bake for 12 minutes.

Makes 36 cookies

optional additions: chopped sun-dried cherries, chopped dried mango (omit chocolate), chopped walnuts or pecans, coconut, sunflower seeds, or dried cranberries

Poppy Seed Oatmeal Cookies

This recipe was originally served at Cantor's Deli in Vancouver. Sheila Cantor generously shared the recipe with me.

¼ cup (60 mL) poppy seeds
¼ cup (60 mL) milk
1 tsp (5 mL) vanilla extract

Soak poppy seeds in milk and vanilla for 2 hours and set aside.

2 cups (500 mL) flour
¼ tsp (1 mL) salt
pinch of soda
1 tsp (5 mL) baking powder

Sift together.

1½ cups (375 mL) rolled oats

Grind until coarse. Add to above; set aside.

½ cup (125 mL) butter
½ cup (125 mL) canola oil

Cream butter and oil.

1 cup (250 mL) brown sugar
⅓ cup (75 mL) white sugar

Gradually add sugars and beat until fluffy.

1 egg

Add and beat until light. Add poppy seed mixture. Add dry ingredients until well blended.

Refrigerate dough for 2 to 3 hours.

Preheat the oven to 350°F (180°C).

Line 2 baking sheets with parchment paper.

Roll onto floured board. Cut into shapes.

Bake on prepared baking sheets in preheated oven for 10 to 12 minutes until light brown.

Makes 48 cookies

Hermit Cookies

These are a Lazy Gourmet invention, designed to be chewy, chunky and hearty.

Preheat oven to 350°F (180°C).

Line 2 baking sheets with parchment paper.

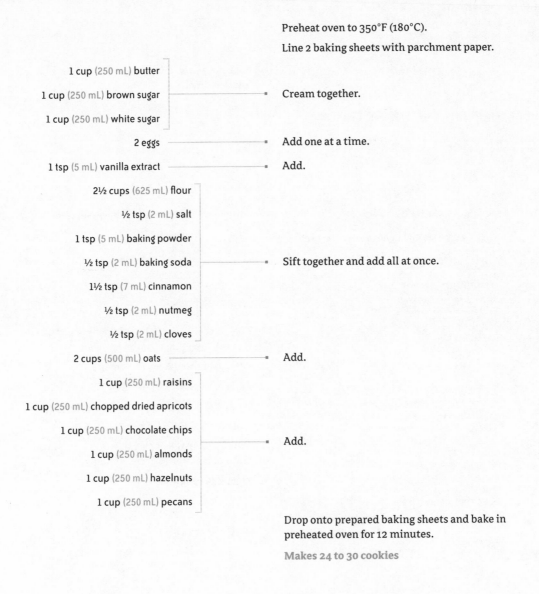

1 cup (250 mL) butter	
1 cup (250 mL) brown sugar	Cream together.
1 cup (250 mL) white sugar	
2 eggs	Add one at a time.
1 tsp (5 mL) vanilla extract	Add.
2½ cups (625 mL) flour	
½ tsp (2 mL) salt	
1 tsp (5 mL) baking powder	
½ tsp (2 mL) baking soda	Sift together and add all at once.
1½ tsp (7 mL) cinnamon	
½ tsp (2 mL) nutmeg	
½ tsp (2 mL) cloves	
2 cups (500 mL) oats	Add.
1 cup (250 mL) raisins	
1 cup (250 mL) chopped dried apricots	
1 cup (250 mL) chocolate chips	Add.
1 cup (250 mL) almonds	
1 cup (250 mL) hazelnuts	
1 cup (250 mL) pecans	

Drop onto prepared baking sheets and bake in preheated oven for 12 minutes.

Makes 24 to 30 cookies

Chocolate Truffle Cookies

I designed this recipe at the lake in an attempt to copy a cookie sold at a small kiosk at Skookumchuk Rapids. It's my most coveted recipe!

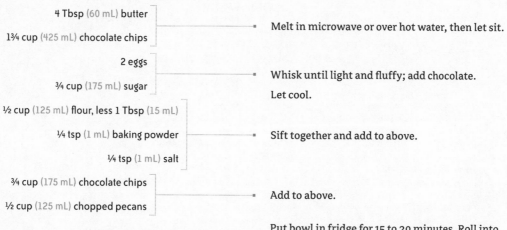

4 Tbsp (60 mL) butter
1¾ cup (425 mL) chocolate chips

Melt in microwave or over hot water, then let sit.

2 eggs
¾ cup (175 mL) sugar

Whisk until light and fluffy; add chocolate.
Let cool.

½ cup (125 mL) flour, less 1 Tbsp (15 mL)
¼ tsp (1 mL) baking powder
¼ tsp (1 mL) salt

Sift together and add to above.

¾ cup (175 mL) chocolate chips
½ cup (125 mL) chopped pecans

Add to above.

Put bowl in fridge for 15 to 20 minutes. Roll into balls; freeze in parchment paper.

Preheat oven to 375°F (190°C). Don't thaw dough. Bake in oven 10 to 11 minutes.

Let sit 5 minutes before moving to cooling rack.

Makes 30 cookies

tip: For added decadence, when the cookies are cooling on the rack, I place 1 square of Lindt 70 percent chocolate on top and watch it melt.

Sheila Cantor's Komish

This is my favorite *komish* recipe. I like to think of them as Jewish biscotti!

Preheat the oven to 350°F (180°C).

Lightly grease a baking sheet.

3 cups (750 mL) flour

1 tsp (5 mL) baking powder

¼ tsp (1 mL) salt

¼ tsp (1 mL) baking soda

Sift together and set aside.

3 egg whites — Beat until peaks form.

1 cup (250 mL) sugar — Add sugar slowly and beat until mixture is consistency of meringue. Set aside.

3 egg yolks

½ cup (125 mL) canola oil

½ cup (125 mL) vegetable shortening

Beat until smooth and buttery-looking.

Fold into egg white mixture.

Fold into flour mixture.

1 cup (250 mL) ground almonds, toasted

⅓–½ cup (75–125 mL) coconut

1 tsp (5 mL) vanilla extract

Fold into mixture.

Mixture should be stiff enough to form 3 rolls.

Place rolls on prepared baking sheet. Bake in preheated oven for 35 minutes. Let cool.

Coating

½ cup (125 mL) sugar

1½ tsp (7 mL) cinnamon

Reduce oven temperature to 200°F (95°C).

Slice the rolls into ½-inch (1-cm) slices and dip in cinnamon-sugar mixture. Turn carefully.

Place coated cookies on cookie sheets in dry oven for at least 2 hours.

Makes 2 dozen komish

Brownies *of the* New Century

If you're going to make a brownie, this is the one that you've been looking for! It's fudgey and chocolatey. For the occasional indulgence. Definitely worth the calories! The recipe was developed by the bakers at The Lazy Gourmet.

Preheat the oven to 350°F (180°C).

Grease a 13- × 9-inch (33- × 23-cm) baking pan, then flour generously.

¾ cup (175 mL) butter

14 oz (440 g) semi-sweet chocolate

Melt butter and chocolate in saucepan over hot water until melted and smooth. Cool slightly.

2 cups (500 mL) brown sugar

4 eggs, lightly beaten

1 Tbsp (15 mL) vanilla extract

Stir sugar and eggs into above. Add vanilla extract.

1 cup (250 mL) flour

1 cup (250 mL) chocolate chips

⅔ cup (150 mL) sour cream

Sift flour and add wet ingredients along with chocolate chips and sour cream.

Pour into prepared pan.

Bake in preheated oven for 35 to 40 minutes. Be careful not to overbake.

cocoa powder

When cooled, dust with cocoa and cut into squares.

Optional Ganache Topping

1 cup (250 mL) whipping cream

8 oz (250 g) semi-sweet chocolate chips or *calets*

Bring cream to a boil. Add chocolate and mix until blended.

Pour over cooled brownies.

Cut into squares when set.

Makes 24 squares

tip: *Calets* are large chocolate chips produced by European chocolatiers.

Crispy Oatmeal Cookies

When you want a simple old-fashioned oatmeal cookie reminiscent of the store-bought Dad's cookie, here it is.

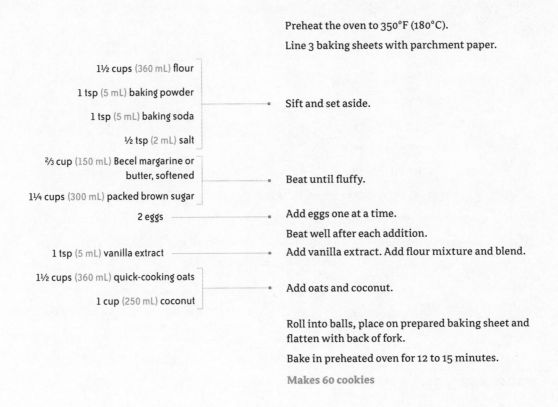

Preheat the oven to 350°F (180°C).

Line 3 baking sheets with parchment paper.

1½ cups (360 mL) flour
1 tsp (5 mL) baking powder
1 tsp (5 mL) baking soda
½ tsp (2 mL) salt

Sift and set aside.

⅔ cup (150 mL) Becel margarine or butter, softened
1¼ cups (300 mL) packed brown sugar

Beat until fluffy.

2 eggs

Add eggs one at a time.

Beat well after each addition.

1 tsp (5 mL) vanilla extract

Add vanilla extract. Add flour mixture and blend.

1½ cups (360 mL) quick-cooking oats
1 cup (250 mL) coconut

Add oats and coconut.

Roll into balls, place on prepared baking sheet and flatten with back of fork.

Bake in preheated oven for 12 to 15 minutes.

Makes 60 cookies

My Favorite Triple Chunk Cookies

A new variation from the recipe in *The Lazy Gourmet*.

Preheat the oven to 350°F (175°C).

Line 2 baking sheets with parchment paper.

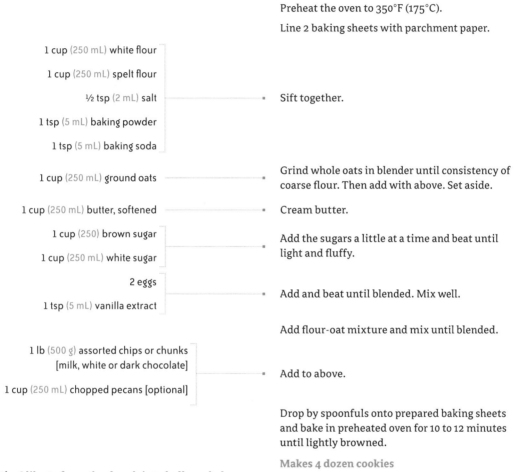

1 cup (250 mL) white flour

1 cup (250 mL) spelt flour

½ tsp (2 mL) salt — Sift together.

1 tsp (5 mL) baking powder

1 tsp (5 mL) baking soda

1 cup (250 mL) ground oats — Grind whole oats in blender until consistency of coarse flour. Then add with above. Set aside.

1 cup (250 mL) butter, softened — Cream butter.

1 cup (250) brown sugar

1 cup (250 mL) white sugar — Add the sugars a little at a time and beat until light and fluffy.

2 eggs

1 tsp (5 mL) vanilla extract — Add and beat until blended. Mix well.

Add flour-oat mixture and mix until blended.

1 lb (500 g) assorted chips or chunks [milk, white or dark chocolate]

1 cup (250 mL) chopped pecans [optional] — Add to above.

Drop by spoonfuls onto prepared baking sheets and bake in preheated oven for 10 to 12 minutes until lightly browned.

Makes 4 dozen cookies

tip: I like to form the dough into balls and place into freezer bags. Then when guests arrive, I bake the frozen dough at 350°F (180°C) for around 14 minutes. It's wonderful to serve fresh hot cookies and great to have the reserved cookies on hand.

Acknowledgements

There are so many people to thank for their input. First, my family has supported me through endless tastings (poor things). Thank you for your patience, gentle criticism and endless support to Jack, Mira, Soleil and Pilar. My sisters and brother have sent many recipes my way. To Rena, Lynn, Freddie and Anita, thanks so much. (Anita, I'm still waiting for that summer salad recipe. It will have to wait for my next book!) Of course, Mama Roz Mendelson has always supported me and cheered me on, just as she did in my growing-up years. I'm eternally grateful and hope that I can be as unconditionally supportive a mom as you have been.

Many thanks to the brilliant and talented staff who work tirelessly every day at The Lazy Gourmet: Shana Aspeleiter, Peter Toynbee, Lisa Blewitt, Yoo Choi, Vita Dixon, Bonnie Chapin and Janet Nixon upstairs and the kitchen, led by Jenny Hui and her fantastic team: genius Gina Naples, Mike Swann, Aviva Black, Dawn Vachon, J.R. Sadian, Pam Shoup, Greg Currie and of course the amazing Aida Gamit, who manages my life, tested my recipes and can even think for me.

The manuscript was first typed by Fanny Whiteley, the second draft by Lisa Page. The editing and final draft was carefully completed by the brilliant Viola Funk. I owe you all a huge debt of gratitude.

To my friends and family who have given me recipes over the years, thank you all, especially Paula Brook (how could I have done it without you?!), Deborah Roitberg, Roberta Niemann, Miriam Gropper, Karen Gelmon, Cousin Sherry Taub, Aunt Naomi Mendelson, Cousin Nancy Posluns, Paige Grunberg, Eve Sheftel, Reva Davidson, my late mother-in-law Miriam Glassman Lutsky and all the others who contributed to the previous nine books and those I've failed to mention. (Being over 50 gives me an excuse for any omissions.)

Food stylist Irene McGuinness and photographer Tracey Kusiewicz were a pleasure to work with. David Robinson needs to be thanked for convincing me to do *Mama Never Cooked Like This* in the first place. Finally, I'd like to thank Robert McCullough, the heart and soul of Whitecap Books, who tasted and tested and prodded and scolded and was ever so charming and understanding as I made my way to the finish line!

Thanks once more to you all.

Index